This Song's for You

This Song's for You

Reva Griffith

Celo Valley Books
Burnsville NC 28714

This book can be ordered by sending $12.50 plus $2.00 shipping to: Reva Griffith, 5745 Charlotte, Kansas City MO 64110.

Cover art by Wanda Knight.
Cover photo by Andrew Sieff.

Library of Congress Catalog Card Number 92-74144
ISBN 0-923687-23-8

Dedicated to

John, my husband, with whom I have walked
for forty-five fulfilling years.

And to

Timothy, Jonathan, and Benjamin,
our three living sons;

Cheri, Jeri, and Patricia,
our daughters-in-law;

Jason, Treva, Alison, Carrie, Jordan,
and newly born Stephanie,
our grandchildren.

Prologue

When someone dear to us dies, we ache to understand death — this mysterious and inevitable piece of the life process that we have known was there all along. The death of a young person seems even more difficult to understand. Why this early, unexpected, seemingly inappropriate interruption of young life? How can we stand it?

One of my reasons for writing this book is to plot one person's journey in "living through" the death of a son, a journey in progress. My hope is that it also will serve as a vehicle of expression for others whose lives Chris touched — a memorial then to Christopher, whose time on this earth ended too soon, but who, while here, attempted to live a thoughtful, sensitive life.

Writing this book has been a very personal way for me to deal with grief. Sometimes, in the early days of writing, words came through a storm of tears. Later, mind and emotion more often merged as I sought to put into words the new places where Chris's death has led and is yet leading me.

For those who grieve, I hope there will be comfort and understanding.

And I hope the readers of this book will learn to love Chris as his family and friends love him.

Acknowledgments

Our gratitude to Chris's friends, patients and co-workers, and to our family and extended family, whose thoughtful, caring words helped write this book.

Special thanks to Alice Winter, who read the words as I wrote them and helped me put them in order.

For what is it to die but to stand naked in the wind and to melt into the sun?

from *The Prophet*
by Kahlil Gibran

Chapter One

Hear ye, hear ye, hear ye, the Circuit Court of Jefferson County is now in session. Judge John L. Anderson presiding. Please be seated and be in order. Thank you.

So intoned the bailiff at 9 A.M., March 21, 1988. The trial of the state of *Missouri* v. *Donald Edward Reese* had begun. Donald Edward Reese was being tried for murder in the deaths of four men; one of these men was our oldest son, Christopher, thirty-eight years old at the time of his death September 9, 1986.

Many years after Christopher's birth, after he had survived an adolescence during the Vietnam War, after he had married and divorced, long after he knew how babies came to be, he asked me, "Mom, where was I conceived?"

Counting the months on my fingers, I said, "Probably in a log cabin in the mountains near Celo, North Carolina."

"Really?" he said, his brown eyes as bright as the North Star. "Really?"

"Yes," I said, "you must have been conceived just before we moved back to Iowa."

He was ecstatic. For that is how he was — awed by the simple things in life.

Today, I never take a serious look at a watermelon without thinking of the evening of July 24, 1948, the evening before Christopher's birth.

My husband, John, and I were living in one middle-sized inelegant room in the heating plant at William Penn College, Oskaloosa, Iowa. The one window (on the south) looked out toward what we at the college called an athletic field. To the east, there was a cinder drive that wound through the college campus. Furnishings in the room included a double bed borrowed from someone, an ancient gas cookstove, a four-drawer dresser and a desk.

There was a wash basin in the room, but the nearest bathing facility was a shower encrusted with nameless crud in the basement of the heating plant where both football players and persons who worked on the buildings and grounds showered. John would stand guard in late evening while I, in pregnant splendor, bathed. The toilet stool in the basement was also available for my use in the evening; during the day I walked the half-block to the main building of the college for restroom facilities. In the latter stages of pregnancy, it was necessary for me to anticipate well ahead of my actual need.

John was in summer school and also employed by the college at a whopping forty-five cents an hour doing building and grounds tasks; in the fall he would assume responsibility for the heating plant.

The evening of July 24 we had been invited to my aunt's house for watermelon. I, with only ten days left until the baby was due, looked as if I were carrying a watermelon of my own. We ate our fill of the chilled, delicious fruit and then we walked home since we had no car. When we arrived back in our room I commented, "Whew, I've eaten so much watermelon my belly's stretching." Only a novice expectant mom would have been so innocent. We were awakened soon after midnight with what I decided might be labor pains. I had been told I would know them when they came and I did, just barely. At 12:30 A.M. we borrowed a car and made our way to the hospital downtown.

Christopher was born at 2:45 A.M., July 25, 1948 at Mercy Hospital in Oskaloosa, Iowa. He weighed 6 lb., 13 oz. Although his "presentation" was somewhat abnormal, it was a quick and fairly painless delivery. His name, Christopher, had been decided upon before his birth by parents who had spent hours poring over lists of names. I liked the lilt of the name and John noted that there was a saint named Christopher — it was an appropriate name for our son. We decided then, and have since regretted this decision, that with such a long name Christopher didn't need a middle name. Later we realized that in not giving Chris a middle name, we had set a precedent for the sons who followed: all four were deprived forever of middle names selected by their parents.

Chris's pleased grandparents were Carl and Isabel Griffith of Greenville, South Carolina, and Arthur and Lydia Standing of Primghar, Iowa.

CHRISTOPHER'S BIRTH

I remember . . .
The day of your birth,
My first born.
I counted your fingers and toes,
Touched your pinkness,
I knew without doubt
You were the most beautiful baby
In the nursery.
No,
In the world.

I looked in the nursery window often,
I, universal mother,
Earth woman.
Had I not nourished you in my womb,
Endured with gladness,
And a little fear,
Your rhythmic, jarring
Journey through my body?

Therefore . . .
I took my place
With all the other mothers
Of the world.
Except that . . .
You were perfect.
— Reva Griffith, 1987

"Mom," Tim said, "Get Dad and put him on another phone. I need to talk to both of you." It was Tim, our second son, who like John and me, lived in Kansas City. I was surprised to hear Tim's voice so late at night when we'd been away from home for only a few hours.

John and I had traveled that day, September 9, 1986, from Kansas City to my parents' home in a Quaker community near Paullina in the northwest corner of Iowa. It had been a pleasant early fall drive up Interstate 29 to Highway 59, a sometimes hilly two lane highway that ran from Missouri past my parents' home just south of the plain white meetinghouse

Chris (six weeks old) with his mother.

in the tiny Quaker community called Mapleside. We were en route to a regional meeting of the American Friends Service Committee being held on the Indian reservation at Pine Ridge, South Dakota. I was a member of the AFSC executive committee, and we had decided, since my mother was not well, to visit her and my stepfather on the way to the meeting.

We had gone to bed at 10:30 that evening, hoping to get an early start the next morning for the rest of our journey. At 12:30 A.M. I was awakened by the ringing of the telephone. As I hurried to the phone, a worried lump stirred in my stomach. I have somehow been programmed to view calls late at night with some anxiety.

To Tim I said, "Your Dad's asleep and I hate to wake him."

"You'll have to," he said, his voice tight and hollow. And I knew then he had a serious message.

My mother and stepfather, looking sleepy and concerned, were already standing with me by the phone. I called John, and then went back to Tim on the phone.

"You'll have to talk with me and then Dad; there's only one phone."

Tim was struggling to control himself as he began to tell an unbelievable story. Only bits registered with me. Officers from the Kansas City police department had tried to locate us and failed. From our neighbors, they had learned where Tim lived. The words I heard were "Chris . . . with friend from the Conservation Department . . . at a firing range . . . interrupted a robbery . . . 4:00 in the afternoon . . . they shot and killed the other man and . . . Chris."

"They killed Chris?" I said, my voice fading. Even now I can remember it sounded peculiar and far away. Oh, no, they couldn't kill Chris. Somehow this could not be true; there had to be a mistake. I leaned against John who took the receiver from me.

Poor Tim — only later did I realize what a painful duty he had performed; he relayed the story to John, who seemed calm but looked as if he had been struck. He told Tim we'd call him back as soon as we had talked.

I began a strange sort of quiet sobbing that scraped at the surface of my feelings. John called the undertaker in Columbia where Chris's body was, found it was too late for any of his organs to be used, that his billfold with possible wishes for disposition of his body was not there, that we could call the university in the morning to find out about donating his body. John told the undertaker we would let him know in the morning what to do.

John and I went to our room and sat on the bed for some minutes before I said, "We'd just as well pack up and start home. We won't be able to sleep. We need to get home and then to Columbia as soon as we can."

John called Tim; we packed and prepared to leave. I went into my mother's room, sorry to give her this burden. In need of her sympathy, I laid my head on her comfortable bosom as I done so often as a child and sobbed. She cried too and with great effort from her failing body put her arms around me. I kissed her good-bye, hugged Dad, and we were off into the night.

The ride home (over three hundred miles) was filled with the sound of the Toyota groaning through the night. Fortunately we found a gas station at Cherokee, thirty miles down the road. There are not many stations open in small Iowa towns that time of night. On the journey, a number of night animals, claiming their right to the darkness, crossed in front of the car — skunks, opossums, groundhogs. Until we reached the interstate in Missouri, we saw no more than a couple of dozen moving vehicles, mostly trucks. We crept through sleeping towns, passed farmsteads dark except for the garish gleam of solitary arc lights in the yards.

We stopped at a truck stop on I-29 where I remember thinking how different the night felt from the carefree day before when we had also stopped there. I wanted to scream out, "Our son has been killed. Help us, help us. How can we bear it?" But we sat there like two tired middle-aged tourists stopping for coffee in the middle of the night on our way to some vacation spot.

As we bore on down the highway, I sometimes felt a sob rise in my throat; we exchanged few words, mostly expressions of disbelief, memories of Chris; our hands were clasped in the space between us on the seat. I meditated on what a satisfactory son Chris was, denying yet that he was gone. And words came to me in the silence of those dark miles, words that were read at Chris's memorial service the following Saturday.

In a way, Chris's life began the day we, his parents, John Harvey Griffith and Reva Paulette Standing, met on the campus of William Penn College in Oskaloosa, Iowa. At that time William Penn College was a liberal Quaker institution whose president, Cecil Hinshaw, espoused peace, racial equality and simple living through a modern day "holy experiment" named for a much earlier attempt at utopian government by William Penn in Pennsylvania.

John and I met during the fall of 1945. I was a shy, serious, Quaker junior, Iowa-born and bred. John, a war resister, had been released only a few months before from two years in prison for refusal to register for the draft. I fell in love at first sight with this tall, handsome, soft-spoken South Carolinian on a search for truth. John, intent on study, work and the meaning of life, didn't notice me for a while. When he did, our courtship was simple. We took long walks, listened to classical music with congenial friends and meditated with a campus group. Once we had an ice cream cone.

Our wedding, a Quaker ceremony, took place at Bear Creek Friends Meetinghouse out in the country near Earlham, Iowa on May 24, 1947. The meetinghouse was located among gently rolling hills, beside freshly plowed fields being prepared for corn planting. With typical Iowa weather whim, the day began with light snow; then a blustery wind chased the snow away and, as if to compromise, the day proceeded with intermittent clouds and sunshine.

I was a birthright Quaker and had spent many quiet, reflective, sometimes rebellious, hours in this meetinghouse with its high ceilings, bare wood floors and walnut benches. John was the son of a Methodist minister who had been a soldier in World War I and whose subsequent study of the economic causes of that war changed him into a man who preached against war. The seriousness with which John, the second son, embraced this message of peace, and his resistance to the draft was a surprise, even to his father.

As we sat there quietly, waiting for the moment to rise and speak our vows, the reality of this love I had chosen set in. My life up until then had pretty much followed the pattern prescribed by the Quaker faith of the time and place where I had grown up; the lifestyle was a mix of rural Iowa and Quaker values. This marriage would bring changes; it was a venture into the unknown. I was sad to leave the security and comfort of this way of life, yet confident of my decision, ready to walk beside John, this seeker of truth.

We rose to say our vows. Holding hands, we — as Friends had done for three hundred years — performed our own wedding ceremony, repeating these vows to one another:

> In the presence of the Lord and these, our friends, I (John/Reva) take thee, (Reva/John) to be my lawful wedded (wife/husband), promising with divine assistance to be unto thee a loving and faithful (husband/wife) as long as we both shall live.

Then we sat down and a certificate verifying our vows was read by my sister, Wanda. There was another period of silence in which sporadic vocal messages were shared. During that time, I'm sure Friends spoke words in support of our decision to marry and wished us well, although I must confess that memories of the words and those who uttered them have gone out of my mind.

The "... these, our friends" spoken of in the marriage vow included relatives, meeting people, community friends and a sizable contingent of staff and students from William Penn College.

I wore a homemade blue shantung dress with a white Peter Pan collar, and John, in keeping with his philosophy of simple living, wore a denim jacket and wash pants. Our garb was unusually plain even for a Quaker wedding. I remember the look of astonishment on the face of my best high school girlfriend as John and I walked into the meetinghouse.

Three days later I graduated from William Penn College and, idealists that we were, we were off to North Carolina by train (my parents couldn't stand the thought of our hitchhiking so they bought us train tickets), full of enthusiasm and energy, to life in a religious community within Celo Community, an "intentional" community.

Celo is located at the base of lofty Mount Mitchell, said to be the highest point east of the Rockies, up the mountain from Asheville, North Carolina. The community, an experiment for testing the small community ideas of Arthur Morgan, the founder of Antioch College, Yellow Springs, Ohio, was made possible through the purchase of land and the construction of a health clinic from money donated by Henry Regnery, a well-to-do Chicago Quaker.

Our home was a shared three-room log cabin, our only private place one room of the cabin. That room was located on the south side of the cabin where we caught a glimpse of the early morning rays of the sun and saw it disappear in a rosy glow behind the mountains in the evenings. As I reflect on my memory of the room, I still have a cozy feeling. It was pleasant in a rustic way — an unvarnished wood floor, a stone fireplace, space enough to accommodate our few belongings. A wooden frame bed constructed by John held the mattress on which we slept.

Arle and Tillie Brooks and their young daughters, Paula and Maryla, occupied the other bedroom; the third room was the kitchen/dining area for all of us. David Jensen, a friend from William Penn College, slept in the attic. We pooled our resources (we're astonished now at our optimistic view of our assets) and lived in common, forming what in the sixties came to be known as a commune; in the forties it was "living a simple life." Furnishings were utilitarian, mostly homemade. Meals were simple; early menus included large steaming bowls of oatmeal with blackstrap molasses for two meals, and for the third, greens and corn bread. There was no electricity or running water in the cabin.

We meditated daily for from two to three hours. In this secluded valley surrounded by the softly rising mountains of the Blue Ridge, we, with sweat of brow and aching backs raised outstanding vegetables for which there was no market.

Another project the men of our group and others in the community conceived and labored to complete was the building of a sawmill. The master plan called for rolling logs downhill to the sawmill. In later years, we have chuckled while viewing the movie *Zorba the Greek* at the similarity in Zorba's ill-fated plan of sending logs down a chute to the sea and the Celo sawmill plan. The result of the plan, for Zorba, was logs bouncing all over the mountain; as failure of the plan became evident, Zorba, ever the optimist, did a carefree dance on the sandy shore. It was probably fortunate we didn't see the fruition of the Celo project; it was abandoned when we discovered the electric motor for the sawmill would cost ten times the estimate! I doubt we would have been as resilient as Zorba; besides there was no soft sand for dancing and certainly no seashore.

Celo was an idyllic place to live. Our water came from a spring; we took our baths in the South Toe River, a stream undefiled by industrial waste and pesticides; juicy wild blackberries grew on the mountainsides. The people in Celo Community were idealists, committed to experimentation with alternative ways of living.

So we lived in this small community with these five other persons in the log cabin; the surroundings were beautiful, the people congenial. However, it became clear to us as time went on that we may not have thought through the difficulties of making a living there. We were aware we might not stay forever.

After six months, we decided to leave. Our decision was not an easy one. We weren't sure we wanted to continue a life of bare subsistence living and we needed time to think it through. Although the community idea still appealed to us, we thought that this one might not be right for us. What tipped the balance toward leaving at the time we did was that my father in Iowa was not well and was retiring from farming. My parents were moving from Earlham, where they had begun their married life over twenty years before to Primghar, Iowa near my mother's girlhood home. They needed some help in making the transition.

At our departure, the whole community joined in a party for us and gave us presents; one plaintive note said, "Stay with us!" Now, as we look back, we see our Celo experience in community living as a valuable episode in our lives. We gained insight into our limitations and strengths as people because we had grown to know, love and at times disagree with the others involved in this utopian venture.

When we visited Celo in the spring of 1990, we understood anew the pull of the simple life. The cabin, tucked back in among the trees, stood there — updated with electricity, running water and additions — a peaceful remnant of times gone by. The South Toe River, sedate, beautiful and still almost pristine, continued on its journey to the sea. With friends living nearby, we remembered the good times.

John and I will always remember Celo as the place where a very special son, Christopher, was conceived in love.

Chapter Two

GENTLE EYES

She said he had gentle eyes,
He did.
Eyes like a doe's;
Large, liquid, brown,
Aware.

And, like a doe,
He was shot down.

He of the gentle eyes.
— Reva Griffith, Sept. 1986

The sun was up the morning of September 10 when John and I arrived back in Kansas City. As we drove into the city, the day looked like any other. The freeway was alive with cars, as people on their way to work sped along toward some unknown destination. On the side streets, yellow buses stopped and started; children, sleep still in their eyes, were on their way to school. Numb with pain, it seemed incredible to us that the world we had left the day before was carrying on as if nothing had happened.

At 8:00 A.M. we were home. We called Tim to tell him we were in town, took showers and changed clothes in preparation for making the incomprehensible trip to Columbia where Chris had lived and where, they said, his body lay.

We then began the task of calling our other sons and members of our families. John broke into sobs when he called Jonathan, our son in Austin, Texas; up until this time, he had been dry-eyed and silent. Jon, and Ben in Frankfort, Kentucky, both assured us they would come soon although their families probably would be unable to do so.

Tim arrived and we embraced and cried together. He brought with him the morning paper which carried the story of the killings. We learned there were four men killed, rather than two. It appeared from the position of the bodies that Chris and Mr. Watson, a Conservation Department safety inspector with whom Chris had been working as a physical therapist, had interrupted a robbery in which two men had already been killed at the firing range near Marshall, Missouri. Mr. Watson routinely stopped there to make safety checks. He and Chris were coming back from a fish hatchery where Chris, in his job as a back pain consultant for Rusk Rehabilitation Center in Columbia, had been exploring ways to lessen back strain for the workers there. The firing range was on their way back to Columbia.

Reading the details didn't help. What had happened didn't feel real. Except for the pain, it seemed as if the story were about someone else.

By 11:00 A.M. that morning, Tim, John and I were ready to leave for Columbia. None of us had slept much the night before, yet we were all wide awake, our minds riveted on this impossible tragedy. John had called a doctor at the university who agreed the university would take Chris's body for research. This was the university where Chris had trained to become a physical therapist; it seemed as fitting as anything we could think of doing. When John called the funeral home, he found the body would be transferred to the university sometime that afternoon for the autopsy.

We arrived in Columbia about 1:30 and went first to the

funeral home where we found Chris's body had already been transferred to the hospital. One of the questions we had each been debating in our minds now had to be faced. If we were able to do so, did we want to go to the hospital to see Chris's body? John didn't want to see the body, feeling Chris was not there; Tim and I both expressed an inclination (in my case, half-formed) to see Chris. But since it seemed likely the autopsy would have already begun, we abandoned the idea. Tim and Penny, Chris's girlfriend, did go to the hospital later but were unable to see the body.

As I look back on this decision, I'm still uncertain as to what would have been most helpful. At the time of my father's death, it seemed evident to me that Daddy was gone with his last breath. After that, his body had little significance for me. I was remembering that; however, it might have seemed more real from the first had we seen Chris. I'm sure John was thinking that the pain of that realization might have been overwhelming, and that a gradual dawning of the horror of it all might be less damaging. I truly don't know which is the better viewpoint.

Days later, as I recorded the happenings of that day, I wrote, "It is puzzling what pictures remain in one's head. I remember walking in the yard of the funeral home. The sun was peeping through thin clouds and a brisk breeze tugged at my hair. I felt like someone else, maybe an actress in a tragic play. I remember thinking how like puppets we were; our very lives had been jerked about and unalterably changed by shots that ended the life of our son. We will never be the same without him."

In October 1947, John and I had moved to my parents' farm home in Iowa where we helped pick corn and get ready for a farm sale. I also spent my early days of pregnancy there, trying to rise above daily morning sickness. My grandmother, who had lived with us since I was eleven, clucked in sympathy,

"I know, I know, lovey," while Mom, who'd never had a day of morning sickness in her life led me to believe she thought I might bear up better. Both viewpoints were useful.

After living with and helping my parents for a couple of months, it was once again time to strike out on our own. John found employment at Quaker Oats — a principled decision since he firmly believed oatmeal was a life staple — in Cedar Rapids, Iowa. We moved to a room in Cedar Rapids where we lived for a month. Then we moved to an apartment in the small Quaker village of Whittier, twenty miles outside the city. John was able to commute from there with others who were employed in Cedar Rapids.

Several months later a plan for the future took shape. As the pregnancy progressed and parenthood loomed before us, we decided it would be a good idea for John to finish work toward a college degree before we made any more decisions. With a degree for John, we would have more flexibility in the choices ahead of us. So in April of 1948 we moved to the heating plant at William Penn College in Oskaloosa, Iowa, where John enrolled in classes for the summer; he also began work with the building and grounds crew.

And Chris was born in July. There's nothing quite like the glow of first parenthood. We found Chris to be superior to the others in the nursery. Indeed, he slept in his crib with seldom a whimper. It was not until a short time after he reached our one-room apartment in the heating plant that he found his voice, and he exercised it with great frequency. We summoned Grandma Standing (my mother), and it helped a lot to have another person to console Chris.

In a week she went home and, on our own once again, we spent sleepless nights listening in helpless stupefaction as our beautiful first-born issued loud and endless complaint. Then, in consultation with the doctor, we tried a supplemental bottle feeding, only to have the milk disappear in a few hungry gulps and the incessant crying stop. He was hungry. I was mortified at my failure to produce enough food for this voracious son. We were to observe often over the years that Chris had a healthy, not-to-be-denied, appetite.

He accomplished the feats of childhood in normal fashion, although the first everything seemed remarkable to us. Neither of us had had much exposure to the rudiments of child rearing. However, there was good old Dr. Spock. His words were as fundamental to us as the Bible to the saved. Generally, our faith was well-founded, although in Chris's case, Spock failed us on at least two counts.

1) On potty training, we were admonished to wait for the leading of the child. We waited. And waited. And waited. Finally, late in his second year, we introduced what is now

Two-year-old Chris in the "backyard" of the heating plant.

called behavior modification. Success at the potty chair brought him a piece of candy corn (we lived in Iowa). That's what it took to be led by that little child.

2) On the bottle, Dr. Spock said, as we remember it, that when a younger child comes into a family, an older child, in an effort to emulate the unwelcome attention getter, may want a bottle again. "Give it to him, he will soon tire of the rubbery taste," said Dr. Spock. Not in Chris's case. He and next younger brother, Tim, went off the bottle at the same time.

Years later, when Chris was a grown-up peace activist in Columbia, Missouri, Dr. Spock came to town with his later gospel, the gospel of peace. Chris was assigned the task of driving Dr. Spock to the airport at the close of his visit. Chris told the good doctor that he was a Spock child. Dr. Spock chuckled and replied that it was not unusual for him to meet young folks of Chris's generation who were raised by the book.

As a child, Chris was somber, serious and dogged in efforts to learn (as in riding his tricycle), or not to learn (as in potty training). He greeted his brothers as they arrived in his life with resignation and some enthusiasm. There were three of them: Timothy (June 10, 1950), Jonathan (April 20, 1952), and Benjamin (October 29, 1954). Chris assumed the elder brother's role with relative ease; he seemed to have an appropriate sense of responsibility for his brothers as well as for himself. This continued until his death.

John graduated from William Penn College in the spring of 1950, after which we spent one year in cold, picturesque Decorah, Iowa (one morning the thermometer stood at forty-seven degrees below zero) where John was a child welfare worker. We then moved to Indianola, Iowa because John had a job with the wholesale farm cooperative, Consumers Cooperative Association, in nearby Des Moines. In Indianola we shared two different houses with my sister and her family, each family finally saving enough money to invest in homes of their own.

Chris started to kindergarten there. However, before his first year of school was out, we moved to Ida Grove, Iowa where John did a year's internship in farm cooperative management training. After that we loaded our belongings and four sons for another move, this time to Napier, Iowa, an unincorporated village of fifty persons, more or less, near Ames, where John managed the Napier Co-op. We didn't move from Napier for fifteen years. Chris finished his public school years there at United Community High School near Boone, graduating in 1966.

For most of the eight years after Chris's birth until our youngest son, Ben, was two years old, diapers flapped on our clothesline several times a week. It was an eventful time in the development of our family.

Many of the details of those busy and engrossing years have escaped our frazzled minds, for if the clothesline was busy, what went on inside and about the house could only be described as perpetual motion. When the boys started to school, there were school activities, followed by long Iowa summers with four barefoot boys clamoring for something to do or someplace to go; there were broken bones and stitches, meals to fix, clothes to launder, a living to be made, a garden to weed and vegetables and fruit to can and freeze to help satisfy the voracious appetites of growing boys.

And then, the teen years were upon us. We had read about adolescence, had at a distant time been adolescents ourselves. I don't believe, though, that anything can prepare a parent for the phenomenon of a normal, toad-carrying lad taking on adolescence. One by one, the boys were transformed into fast-growing, secretive, awkward boy-men trying to find their ways through a morass of changes in themselves, their peers and the world about them, preferably without our willing help. This happened in the troubled sixties and early seventies, and it was enough to knock two conscientious parents a little silly. It was a harrowing time. We all made it, barely, though not unscathed, and carried on.

The following poem, written a few months after Christopher's death, tells of those years and the years after:

FOUR BROTHERS

There were four of them,
Four brothers.
They grew like steps,
Each taller than the other.

I see them romping in the sun,
Like playful pups they tumble
In the grass;
I see them fall,
Their bleeding knees
And damaged pride
And tears
Made better by a kiss.

I see them sleeping in their beds,
Their faces touched
With dreamy innocence.

The days were short,
Full,
Too quickly gone.

One by one
As locusts molt,
Their childhoods dropped.
They dreamed their dreams,
Stepped forth
Into a crazy world
Of war and pain unhealed
By tears and kisses.

Then, four men they were
Tall and lean as elms
Searching for their way,
Somber, hopeful, wiser.

And then there were three,
The oldest murdered
By the bullet of a madman.

And I have seen their tears
And know their great love
For their fallen brother.
— Reva Griffith, January, 1987

So Chris's youth was spent there in the middle of Iowa with his family. We lived in an old-fashioned white frame house. Behind the house, on the other side of the fence marking the end of our backyard, was a field which alternately produced corn and beans from some of the richest soil in the world. And on cloudless and near cloudless days, summer and winter and in-between, the sun slipped over the horizon behind that field in a gaudy array of color. It was a quiet, mostly peaceful place, where children played outdoors

"Four Brothers"

together all year round, tossing the balls appropriate to the season. It was where Chris grew from child to youth and where there were enticing flashes of the man he would become.

The Griffiths, 1957.

Parents: Reva and John, and sons: Chris, Tim, Jon and Ben.

Chapter Three

I see them romping in the sun,
Like playful pups they tumble
In the grass;
I see them fall,
Their bleeding knees
And damaged pride
And tears
Made better by a kiss.

from *Four Brothers*
by Reva Griffith, January, 1987

Who was Chris as a child? As a teenager? A young person? Like all of us, Chris, the youth, foreshadowed Chris, the adult. This part of the Chris story comes from memories of some of us who knew Chris well as a child and young person.

Photos

Soon after Chris's death, I talked of collecting photos of him. I had a vague plan, loosely articulated as was everything in those sorrowful days, of putting together a photo album. Tim, our Hallmark employee son, made it easier by presenting me with a new Hallmark photo album. After that, I spent many days that first Chris-less winter buried in photos — collecting, organizing, getting reprints, labeling, and finally, making a photographic history of Chris. Now as I thumb through the pages, memories of Chris as he was growing up swirl back.

There are photos of the six-week-old Chris — not much hair, a hint of a cleft chin, darkish looking eyes when they are open. He lies in our arms, tranquil, a Buddha-like picture of repose, a little misleading, given the hours we remember walking around that one-room apartment with crying baby in our arms.

When Chris was ten months old, we splurged on a roll of colored film so that John's family in South Carolina could see our first-born in living color. Now the two remaining colored photos of Chris at that age are yellow and faded. In one, Chris sits in his stroller wearing a denim jacket and cap I made, gazing back at the camera, thoughtful and somber; below the picture I have written, "Smile? Not me!" In the other, our heating plant home in the background, he stands on sturdy ten-month-old legs, a pair of overalls hiding his feet, in a meditative pose, his reddish hair coiffed into a curl. This shot is captioned, "Jes' thinking."

Photos, even then, show a serious, reflective child, although there are exceptions — like the one of a mellow, smiling Chris petting a black kitty. And in another, Chris, seven months old, stands holding onto the side of his crib in the corner of our one-room apartment, laughing at something, probably foolish gyrations of parents on the other side of the camera. Then later, there is two-year-old Chris, a devilish grin on his face, pulling his baby brother Tim in a little red wagon. One wonders whether the scab on Tim's forehead might have been the result of a reckless ride the day before. And then, later yet, as we got a new camera and moved into colored slides, ten-year-old Chris, shirtless, is on his stomach on the living room floor with Ben, then three, astride his back; both look very happy.

As he grew older, photos of Chris by himself were rare (as were solo photos of any of the subsequent sons). More often, all of the current children are pictured together. In many of these photos, Chris looks like the older brother, responsible, a bit above the clowning and restlessness sometimes exhibited by the younger ones. Usually he wears a happy expression although broad grins are uncommon.

However, there is a snap of a very new Jonathan being held by smiling, proud Chris; Tim, appearing a bit uneasy, pats the baby's head while a piece of Daddy John supervises from the edge of the picture. Some of the photos, seemingly

Chris pets the kitty.

simple snaps of cooperative children, bring back memories of begging, cajoling, even bribing, first two, then three, and finally four, busy little boys to stand still for just a few seconds. Had I known time would slip by so quickly, I would surely have been more patient.

Then there are school photos, snapshots with cousins or friends, newspaper pictures of the basketball star, prom photos showing a tall, handsome young man in a tux, and finally graduation. They plot the growing up of young Christopher.

Curly auburn baby hair is trimmed and replaced by butch haircuts superseded by flattops, then by a gradual lengthening of hair until the high school graduation photo of a serious Chris, hair parted and combed neatly over to the side. In the two or three years following graduation, the hippie craze caught up with Chris and photos of the Chris of that era often show an incredible mass of auburn hair, sometimes with an equally astounding matching auburn beard. But that comes later.

Flashbacks

I have tried to think of ways to reconstruct a brief story of young Chris and have concluded that the job of being parents is so absorbing, and so many things happen, often simultaneously, that remembering comes only in snatches. Perhaps as the memories unravel in my old age, I can tell a more comprehensive story of Chris and his brothers.

For now I think in pieces. When I think of Tim, I think of a mischievous elf of a child with a grin, dancing eyes and lots of freckles. Jon was a smiling baby with blond curly hair and blue eyes; casual passersby glanced at him with admiration. Ben appears as a dark-eyed, intent four-year-old determinedly taking off from the back steps in an effort to ride his brother's bike. Calling up any of these images can start a train of memories that leap about in hit-and-miss fashion.

And what of their older brother, Chris? The same pattern

emerges. Flashes of memory. Some of these memories, augmented by help from family and friends, follow. They don't tell the whole story; rather, they are like the shapes and colors on an impressionist's canvas — they give us an idea of who Chris was in his youth.

#1. We are in a hamburger/sandwich joint somewhere in Tennessee on our way to visit John's family in South Carolina. The year? Maybe mid-summer of 1962; this would make Chris 12, Tim 10, Jon 8, and Ben, almost 6. We sit at a round table in the center of the restaurant. We are relieved to be indoors where there is air conditioning, out of the stifling heat of a crowded car that is air conditioned only by gusts of hot air blowing (all too seldom) through open windows. And we are hungry.

For miles, the boys have demonstrated a growing unrest. We have heard cries ranging from "I'm hungry" to "Dad, stop, I have to go to the bathroom real bad." From the pilots' seats, we've been trying to ignore the mutinous rumblings, uttering a cheerful, "Just a few more miles to a town" or a desperate "Who can win the ABC's game?" or, as the complaining grew, a loud "Sit down and be quiet or else . . ."

Now we all pore over the menus (one makes careful selections when restaurant visits are infrequent). After a suitable interval, Tim, Jon and Ben select hamburgers and French fries, a predictable choice. Chris, who had a meatless diet as a young child (his parents had been vegetarians then), still ponders; he doesn't like meat very well, he's hungry, he wants to get what he wants the most. The waitress, pad in hand, is staring out the window at the cars passing by.

"Hurry up, Chris, we're starving," says Jon.

"Yeah, just order a hamburger and be done with it," from Tim.

"I'm hungry," Ben whines.

"Time's up," John adds.

In desperation, Chris orders French fries and a grilled cheese sandwich. The waitress notes the order on her pad and turns to leave.

With hesitation, Chris asks, "Is it Velveeta?"

Tim and Jon moan "Oh Chris"; Ben echoes "Oh Chris." The waitress stops, puzzled.

John waves her on. Once again, she turns to leave.

We sigh and start to relax. All except Chris. As the waitress takes her first step, he says, "Wait. Can I ask you something?"

Our eyes focus on Chris; he looks hesitant and uncomfortable.

"Yes?" says the waitress, clearly vexed.

"Could you bring ketchup?"

She nods and turns again toward the kitchen.

Then he asks, "Is it Del Monte?"

#2. John and I rap on the car window, begging, "Come on out, Chris. It's time to go. We'll be late."

"I don't want to go." A veiled twinkle in his eye.

"You're keeping the rest of us from going."

"I don't care." He is inside and we are outside, locked doors between us. He has the keys. He is in control. We are frustrated and helpless.

It is Sunday morning and we are ready to go to Quaker meeting (church). Chris is six years old and Ben a small baby; Tim and Jon are in-between.

For a while we stand around the old black-and-white Dodge in our meeting-best, ready to go, confident he will give up, watching Chris in the car as if he were a monkey in a cage. John and I implore him to be sensible and open the door; he refuses, his dark eyes unrelenting. It doesn't take Tim and Jon long to recognize a good thing and they are off to play.

When it is obvious we are not going to meeting, John,

looking grim and every bit as stubborn as his eldest son, calls Tim and Jon, takes them by the hand, strolls to the neighborhood Dairy Queen, buys a nickel cone (our limit in those days) for each and comes back, Tim and Jon happily lapping ice cream. For just an instant, Chris grabs the door handle, about to weaken; then, as if coming to his senses, he jumps into the back seat, plants himself in the middle and from there, somberly peers out at the ice cream lappers. I don't remember when he gave up.

#3. Chris enters the stage at the junior high school with his pianist, a girl in his class. It is the monthly PTA meeting, a significant event in this small, rural community, and Chris has been asked to play a cornet solo. He is nervous but prepared. In eighth grade and tall for his age, decked out in a new brown suit, his hair painstakingly combed, he makes an impressive entrance. He glances at his music stand; it is empty. With a look of panic he rushes to his pianist and thumbs through her music. His music isn't there. He rushes offstage, clutching his cornet, returning in a short time with a smile and the music.

A kind neighbor whispers to me, "Really, he doesn't need to play at all. He looks so handsome; all he needs to do is just stand there." I'm glad he played; he played well.

#4. We are on a long weekend family visit to Chicago. We are trying to broaden our children's horizons with an educational trip; recreational incentives are thrown in. This morning we are visiting the Museum of Science and Industry — an educational piece of the package. As we near the gate, Chris and Tim decide they need to go to the restroom first.

We assure them that will be fine; they don't have to pay to get in.

"It's okay," we say, "you get in free. See the sign says children twelve and under get in free."

We go on in with Jon and Ben and begin to wend our way through the museum. A few minutes later, Chris and Tim catch up with us. Chris has an aggrieved look on his face.

"What's wrong?" we ask.

"Well, when I told the man I was twelve, he said, 'Kid, you're lyin'!' Then he said, 'Aw, go on in,' but he looked mad."

(Of our four sons, Chris had the shortest, fastest adolescent growing spurt. At the beginning of the year he was twelve, he was five feet, six inches tall; at the end of that year, he was six feet tall. The trip to Chicago took place near the end of that year.)

#5. John and I are at Iowa State University at a concert of the St. Louis Symphony. We would have preferred not to be there that evening. Chris, a high school freshman, is on the high school basketball squad and he has told us that he might get to start the game. Of course, we would have been delighted to forego the concert in order to see him play.

"No," he'd said, "I want you to go to the concert. It'll make me nervous to have you there."

So here we are, rather unwillingly. The orchestra is playing a Dvořák symphony. In the middle of one of the movements, a voice from the public address system breaks in and the orchestra abruptly ceases playing.

"John Griffith," the voice says, "please come to the office; there is an emergency." Frightened, we stumble and fumble our way in the dark to the aisle. We learn in the office that Chris is in the emergency room at the hospital; there is no information as to what is wrong. We hurry to the hospital, fearful of what we may find. What we find is that hospital authorities need our permission to take Chris to surgery to set a dislocated shoulder.

What a relief! We learn later that the conductor, frustrated by the interruption, broke his baton. This anecdote from an experience that had the feel of tragedy was amusing at the time. The tragedy was yet to come.

More about Chris and sports: As a youth, Chris loved sports, especially baseball and basketball. He collected baseball cards, amassing two shoeboxes full; he never quite forgave me for giving them to a cousin when we moved from Iowa, long after he had been a resident son. While watching sports on television occupied some of his time, his major interest was participation in sports. In our small town, the Griffith boys and their friends spent many hours playing baseball, basketball, volleyball, and football in the schoolyard across from our house.

In high school, he played first base on the team from the time he was a freshman; he had watched pro teams and knew where to be to back up plays so he did a good job of fielding. Hitting was not a strong point, although with his usual determination, he worked hard at it.

He excelled in basketball. As a player, he had finesse, knew how to move on the floor. Probably the characteristic that kept him from being outstanding was a lack of aggressiveness; he was not a blood-and-guts person, even playing basketball. But he had many fine moments on the basketball court.

#6. It is a dark and moonless Halloween night. Chris and two of his friends are riding around in a car belonging to one of them. As they cruise down the blacktop about ten o'clock, one of them (not Chris, of course) has an idea of throwing a pumpkin at a car they are about to meet. The pumpkin lands on the radiator of the other car with a splat.

There is a screech of brakes as the person in the other car turns around and chases them down the road. For a mile or so, they are ahead; then good judgment overcomes them and they pull over to the side of the road.

Much to Chris's chagrin, the driver of the other car is a young man who works for John at the co-op.

#7. We approach the intersection of highways 69 and 30 in Ames. I am in my role as driving instructor. Chris, with a new driving permit — my first pupil — is driving. For some unfathomable reason, I have let him drive in town with the other three boys in the back seat.

There is a stoplight at the intersection. The light turns green and we need to turn left; with a start, I realize my student needs instruction. The problem is one of judgment; how quickly can he maneuver a left turn into oncoming traffic?

I hesitate and then decide the time is right.

"Okay, go," I say. He starts; I waver. "No, don't go." He stops and I waver again. "No, it's okay, go."

By now, my already nervous student, is very anxious. He goes. And in the final throes of a nerve-wracking turn, he loses control and we bounce up onto the curb.

Drivers of passing autos crane their necks in surprise. As for the passengers in the back seat, there are a few moments of astonished silence before they break into noisy and hysterical laughter. Chris, manfully holding back tears, is in no condition to continue his stint at the wheel. We quickly change places. I maneuver the car off the curb and head toward home, apologizing to Chris all the way for my herky-jerky judgment. He is embarrassed, but, characteristic of Chris, he doesn't blame me.

Chris did get his license; as the oldest in the family, he was the first to get that much-coveted teen possession. Tim, two years younger than Chris, rode with him to the Boone County Fair on his first night drive without either parent. Tim says, ". . . Going to the fair, Chris drove like a model citizen. However, on the way back from the fair he really got a taste of his newfound power. I'll never know if it was an accident — or how much of an accident it was — but at one stop he took off and laid about twenty feet of rubber. He acted as if it had been intentional."

#8. We are at the beach in a house belonging to John's brother, Bob. It is lunchtime and all eighteen of us (Granddaddy, Grandmommie, Bob, John, Bill and families) are gathered around the table on the back porch. From the porch-side of the house we look out on a tidal creek; we can hear the rhythmic pounding of the surf from the ocean-side (the front) of the house.

With ravenous beach appetites we look at the feast Grandmommie has prepared. We are waiting for the blessing usually asked by Granddaddy or one of his sons.

But that day Bob says, "Chris, you ask the blessing today."

Chris, in early adolescence, looks surprised. He is accustomed to the traditional Quaker blessing, a few moments of silence. He has never verbally asked a blessing in his life.

Red of face and tongue-tied, he finally stammers, "Oh, Father God . . ." and gets no further as our three other sons, and Chris, burst out laughing.

More about the beach: We spent a week of every other summer on the South Carolina beach. John's older brother, Bob, had bought a beach house from a nervous owner not long after Hurricane Hazel. He generously shared the house with the whole family during that one week. All of us remember those times of being beach folk with fondness and gratitude.

When the children were young, they immersed themselves in the innocent pursuits available at the beach — swimming, building sand castles, hunting shells, catching crabs and fish, playing exhausting games of volleyball on the beach, boating, and so on. However, there came a time when that was not enough, especially at night.

Bob Griffith III, twenty-five days older than Chris, remembers: "When Chris and I were about fifteen or sixteen, during one of our family vacations we slipped out of the house at night, along with Tim, by climbing down a ladder from the second floor window. We stayed out late and got nailed the second or third night. John told us not to repeat our carousing. I was moderately persuasive when it came to painting a glowing picture of wine, women and song and Tim was a manipulator of right and wrong without peer. However, neither of us could persuade Chris to slip out again."

Other Memories

Jonathan Remembers ... "The main thing I remember about Chris as a child was how studious he was, really the most studious among us. He was serious about studying, and band, and sports, and choir. The one funny thing I remember was that he saved his allowance in a cigar box until he had enough to cash it all in for a twenty-dollar bill. Typically, the rest of us spent our allowance as fast as we got it."

School Days ... Chris's cousin, Joyce Osborn, writes: "In high school, Chris was popular, and the most memorable thing to me was that he was kind and considerate of everyone. In our class, there was an in-crowd and an out-crowd and a few of us that were in-between. Chris basically associated with the in-crowd but sort of floated within all the groups. He didn't laugh at Jerry's stuttering or Betty's clothes [not their real names] — even at that time, he was more concerned with each person as an individual ..."

Cousins ... Chris's Aunt Wanda (my sister) writes: "... It was exciting watching the cousins grow and develop together — they were all so different yet there was love and caring going on. ... I always felt good when Chris was around when Ben and Pauli were little; he seemed to feel responsibility for them that the others didn't always feel. He was tender with little Nicholas and thrilled with Tom."

Mary Fuller, a Griffith first cousin, writes, "Unfortunately, my memories of Chris as a youth are not very detailed. He was four years older and a boy so we never really spent much

Chris, graduation photo, 1966, United Community High School, Boone, IA.

time together. However, I do have very strong memories of his kindness. I remember not feeling threatened by him and that he was a friend."

Good-bye to Youth

Chris graduated from United Community High School in 1966 in the top ten percent of his class. On graduation night, he and his classmates, looking young, vulnerable and proud, marched into the school gymnasium wearing the maroon caps and gowns of the school. As the strains of *Pomp and Circumstance* rang in our ears, we felt proud of this tall, serious young man, our oldest son.

Although Chris did a good job of applying himself to whatever task was at hand, he also had good times with his friends. He dated some during his high school years although preoccupation with music, sports and getting good grades prevented extensive dating. And for some reason, especially where girls were concerned, he lacked self-confidence.

During high school, he continued to be as responsible as one could expect a teenager to be. Of course, there were lapses, but they weren't serious; at least if there were serious lapses, we don't know of them. There seemed to be something of a breaking away from family after the senior trip to the Ozarks at the end of the school year. I suppose it was time for Chris to begin testing the values he had grown up with and to formulate some of his own.

Chapter Four

OH
A falling star . . .
The banshee squalls,
The lover bows low
To lost rainbows.

Look, you will see
Love's honesty
Saying so clear
That death is near,

To you everyone,
So dance in the sun,
The day has come,
The dew is done.

from *The Sun It Rises*
a song by Chris Griffith

The rest of that day in Columbia (September 10, the day after Chris's death) is a painful blur. I am glad I made some notes a few days later or I might have blocked it out altogether.

We phoned Chris's Columbia friends, many of whom had called us at home that morning, agreeing to meet Penny,

Chris's girlfriend, and Bill, a close friend, at Chris's house. As we got out of our car at 4200 Rock Quarry Road, they met us in the yard where we consoled one another, unable to make sense out of this event that had taken the life of one so conscientious, gentle and caring. We were grateful for Bill and Penny's support as we began to put together what remained of Chris's life and to deal with the pain of his death.

We didn't know where to start. We didn't know what we needed to do; we hadn't done this kind of thing before. So we each latched onto something. Tim took care of arranging for utility cut-off and bills. John and I went to the bank to see what needed to be done about Chris's bank accounts; we were treated with utmost courtesy and a tenderness we hadn't expected. We went to Rusk Rehabilitation Center to pick up Chris's things and to speak with his friends at work. It was obvious they too suffered pain at the death of this special, caring co-worker.

Detectives from a special law enforcement group working on the murder case visited us at Chris's house in the late afternoon. They were considerate as they inquired about Chris, his habits, his past, who he was. We answered their questions, feeling all the while as if we were either talking about someone else or that Chris was lost and these men would surely find him as they searched for clues. At that point, who had committed the crime was of little concern to us — what was of concern was that Chris was gone.

In the early evening we went to the parking lot where Chris had left his silver Toyota wagon, a car he had selected with such care that we all thought he would never get it. There it was, one of the few possessions Chris, an inveterate tightwad, had bought brand-new. Later I wrote this poem about Chris's Toyota:

THE SILVER TOYOTA

Today you should have gone to work
In your silver Toyota

Where, with your well-trained hands
You'd ease the pain of an aching back,
And exchange quips with your co-workers,
Or plan a workshop,
Or look in on an ailing child.
Then after work
You should have met your friends
For a quiet evening of conversation.
Or singing.
Or you should have taken a solitary walk
By the creek you showed us once.
Or have met with your men's group
To discuss the problems of your sex.
Or with your special girl
You should have taken that silver Toyota
You so carefully chose
Out on a country road
Where you could see the moon rise
And the stars appear
In a dark and murky sky,
And hear the mournful call of an owl
Over the wooded hills.

But you can't do these things
Because one day you went to work,
Parked your silver Toyota in the lot,
And, with an acquaintance,
Innocently went about your job.
And met your death
At an ugly firing range.
Suddenly, violently.
All unplanned for
By even the angry one
Who shot you
And the others.

I often think of the days after
When we, with aching hearts,
Gathered the scattered belongings
Of your life —
Your clothes, the furnishings of your house,
Your special trinkets,
Treasured tapes and records.
And your silver Toyota
That should today be
Parked in the lot at your work.
— Reva Griffith, April 1987

At the parking lot, Tim got into Chris's car and we went to Forrest's home — Forrest was another good friend of Chris's — where many friends had gathered. There we were showered with food, love and tenderness. They told us of their love for Chris, of their sorrow at his death, and they offered to help us in any way they could; agreed, in cooperation with the Columbia Friends Meeting, to help plan the memorial service to be held the following Saturday. One of the memories that touches me deeply about this gathering is of a young woman, Candida League, who hugged me and said, "I loved him too." Candida died in 1989.

Later that same evening we started the journey home, stopping once when Tim needed gas for the wagon. It seemed like years had passed since the midnight call that had told of Christopher's death — years of a bad dream of driving and talking and driving again. But it was still only ten o'clock — less than twenty-four hours had gone by.

I wrote later, "I was impressed with John and his ability to think under this kind of pressure, an ability, perhaps innate, perhaps a result of his years in business. I was grateful for Tim there beside us, taking charge when John would let him (more often as the day wore on), giving much needed encouragement, all the while grieving alone as only a brother can grieve. At least John and I had each other."

We fell into bed that night, heavy-hearted, and woke the following morning with the same heavy hearts, both of us sobbing, our hands clasped.

> Back in the sixties we were mighty cool,
> We broke all the goldurn rules,
> When Uncle Sam said I want you,
> We told him a thing or two.
>
> from *Back in the Sixties*
> a song by Chris Griffith

After graduation from high school in the spring of 1966, Chris was uncertain about what he wanted to do but aware that Vietnam and the draft made some kind of decision necessary. So that fall he started to Iowa State University in Ames, six miles from home. His declared major, more or less pulled out of the hat, was sociology. Instead of living at home, he decided to live in one of the men's dorms on campus. He came home frequently, bearing dirty clothes and lots of books.

He didn't live in the dorm long before he decided the distractions of dormitory living were too great. We (especially his father) had encouraged an adventure away from home although having our first-born fly from the nest, even such a short distance, was rather traumatic. We didn't encourage, or expect, the next move. He and John Eveland, one of his best friends from high school who also attended the university, hit upon the idea of joining a fraternity. They said they thought they needed the discipline provided by the brothers. Surprised at this turn of events, we went along with his decision although it was certainly not something we would have desired for either ourselves or Chris.

His friend and cousin, Nancy Osborn, later expressed her feelings about this move in these words: "... The fact that he'd joined a fraternity seemed so incongruous somehow to the rest of his values, and I know I felt at the time that this was one way he was seeking out and testing 'the system' and at the same time making a statement and testing who he really was."

There was discipline at the fraternity, probably not exactly the kind Chris and John had in mind. Though studying was encouraged, so were social events and proper dress, neither of great concern to Chris.

At the fraternity, Chris, apparently feeling independent and grown-up, grew a beard. The beneficiary of his father's healthy hair gene, even at the young age of nineteen he proved he was capable of growing a conspicuous beard — thick and auburn and all over his face. The brothers in charge asked him to please shave his beard. When he didn't do it, he was told he must shave his beard. Here the stubbornness noted earlier became evident. Our memories are fuzzy as to what exactly took place after that, though we do remember he made some sort of appeal to someone higher up than the brothers and was allowed to keep the beard. As soon as he won his case, he shaved. The remainder of the year at the fraternity was not pleasant for Chris; he had established himself as someone who might get out of step.

Which he did. During that year Chris and his friend, John, got involved with the radical Students for a Democratic Society. His cousin, Joyce, recalls a time when a group of SDS'ers were distributing anti-war pamphlets outside churches on Sunday morning. At one of the churches Chris hit upon the idea of assisting people out of their cars and steering them toward his friends who waited nearby with pamphlets, a maneuver that did not increase the popularity of the local SDS.

It was obvious the choices he was making did not distinguish him as good fraternity material. In that time of foment, even Iowa State, traditionally a school of proper, conservative, upcoming farmers and engineers, awoke from a quiet dream. For it was while Chris was at Iowa State University that Don Smith, a bearded hippie with a radical platform pledging to "drag Iowa kicking and screaming into the twentieth century," was elected president of the student body. Chris was pleased with this turn of events.

With the war in Vietnam heating up, Chris decided the next year to go to the University of Iowa in Iowa City where there was an atmosphere more accepting of radical ideas. This time he majored in English and became a hippie. He and his cousin, Ron, and others, lived in a cabin near the reservoir just outside Iowa City. We were never sure just who all lived there. It occurred to us to ask more questions, but like most liberal parents of the Vietnam era, we still tried to trust our offspring in spite of misgivings. We might have been less trusting had we been aware of all the forces at work in the radical world our children were falling into.

The next few years are years many of us would like to forget — though we do glance back at them with a strange nostalgic fascination. Chris didn't talk much about what was going on with him although we were aware, as parents often are, that he was struggling with some absorbing problems, problems many young men his age struggled with during that time. Where did he stand on the draft? On drugs and sex? Politics and war? We stood by, as we did with all four sons in those years, viewing the plethora of possibilities for bad decisions with anxiety, hoping somehow that our fumbling efforts in the years up until then to furnish our sons with something solid upon which to build would provide them with more than a useless, shifting pile of rocks.

At the beginning of his junior year, Chris moved to an apartment in town. His next younger brother, Tim, remembers, "When Chris and I both lived in Iowa City, for a time we lived in the same apartment building. I think we really got close for the first time. We used to eat dinner together and alternate cooking and location. He always cooked Spanish rice and I always cooked spaghetti with mushrooms. (He was vegetarian then.) It took quite a few years before I enjoyed either dish again. Sometime within the last year or two of his life we talked about this time, and Chris confessed to a similar reaction. We were both emotionally in bad shape back then and these dinners were safe harbors."

At the end of his junior year, Chris decided to go to California, not an uncommon adventure for a hippie in those days. We were concerned about him because he seemed depressed and confused, but again, we let him go. I remember taking him to Ames where he was to catch a ride to California with some friends. As he got out of the car with his ragtag bundle of possessions, I felt such deep anguish, I could hardly bear it. I got out and stood beside the car; he kissed me, and moved away. His eyes, dark and sad, looked out from a face surrounded by a bright rim of unkempt beard. As he turned back toward me, he said, "Bye, Mom," and there was regret in his voice. I truly wondered, given what I perceived his state of mind to be, if we would ever see him again. I wrote a poem later that day expressing my feelings about his departure.

RELEASE

As you walk away from me,
I stand, smile pasted on my face.
Gusty breezes tug at your long auburn hair,
Your tall body bends into the wind,
Tangled beard giving you the look
Of a prophet.

Inside, I cry, "Come back."
So much unsaid, undone.

At the corner you disappear.
I turn; the smile drops,
Splattering on the pavement
In a million tears.

— Reva Griffith, 1969, 1990

At first we heard from him infrequently. That was not a good sign. When the letters did come, they were not very reassuring, although as John observed in a piece he wrote concerning this time, "Chris's desire to avoid deception and still not hurt those he loved was evident in these letters." He made it clear that he was involved in the hippie culture, yet at the same time "we always felt assurance that he cared deeply for family and friends . . ."

Then letters, more frequent and more like Chris, started to come. He had met a young woman named Susan from Pittsburgh, Pennsylvania. They were both confused about their lives; it seemed that together they were making some sense out of it all in that crazy mixed-up time.

> . . . I remember the first Christmas Chris and I had, in California. We got a tree and made ornaments out of colored paper, and made Christmas cards. The cat I adopted which everyone hated (with good reason) climbed the tree and demolished the whole thing
>
> — Susan, December 1988

Chris did return from California — twice. The first time, early in 1970, he came back in response to a summons from his draft board for a physical. Not being in school had caught up with him.

John tells of an incident on this visit. "I had just taken a new job in Kansas City developing cooperative housing for limited income families. I had a room at the YMCA, and the firm I worked for had offices in a downtown Kansas City bank building. Reva, Jonathan and Benjamin remained in our home near Ames, planning to stay there until the end of the school year at which time they would join me in Kansas City.

"Chris decided to visit me in Kansas City on his way from California back to Iowa. He arrived there early one evening. Although Chris had begun rejecting society's standards for proper personal appearance before he went to California, I was not prepared for the Chris I met. It appeared he had not cut his hair or trimmed his beard for months and his clothes were badly in need of the washing machine. However, he met me with a huge grin and a bear hug, and his eyes and voice told me plainly that he loved me and was glad to see me. After recovering from the initial shock of his appearance, I was able to see and feel the sensitive and caring Chris behind the wild appearance and we had a good evening together, talking late into the night.

"The next morning Chris was to catch a bus leaving for Ames at 10:00. We had breakfast together and I suggested I would drop him off at the bus depot on my way to work at 9:00. At this point, Chris said, 'Say, Dad, why don't you show me where you work before I catch the bus?' The thought immediately flashed through my mind, 'What in the world will my new co-workers think if I take this wild looking man into our office and say this is my son?' I hesitated a moment and said something to the effect that my office was like a hundred other offices he had seen: a desk, a telephone, a calculator, a couple of chairs and some files with about a dozen co-workers similarly outfitted for business.

"In retrospect, I feel certain of two aspects of this experience: first, Chris had no idea how 'shocking' his appearance would be to my co-workers, and second, he saw right through my deception. He paused a moment and with a big smile he threw his arm around my shoulder and said, 'Hey, no sweat, Dad. Let's just go to the bus depot.'

"That's what we did. Now I wish I had taken Chris to my office, put my arm around him and proudly announced to my well-dressed co-workers, 'I would like to introduce my son, Chris.' I didn't do that. But I know I am forgiven."

Then it was time for the rest of us to welcome Chris back to Napier. We were happy to see him once again. Chris however, was worried about the draft physical. Although he had conscientious objector status, he felt he didn't want to do alternative service in a war like the one raging in Vietnam. That would certainly have been the least stressful thing to do.

Instead, he wrestled with a conscience concerned over many aspects of the draft. What of equally sincere men who were not granted C.O. status? What of the selective objectors to the Vietnam war? What of those who didn't believe in war but were not religious objectors? Was it honest to do any kind of service in light of the war taking place in Vietnam? For him, it was not just that he personally did not believe in killing; it was all these other things too. We'll never know all the options he considered. Reluctantly, he took the physical and then returned to Susie in California.

A short time later Chris and Susie came to Iowa together, and for a while lived with us in Napier. Chris seemed more settled. Like many young men his age who survived the Vietnam era, he retained certain aspects of the hippie look although the serious, friendly Chris, looking older and wiser, was definitely back.

We liked Susie immediately. She had been an art major at Peabody Institute in Baltimore before going to California where she and Chris had met at the home of a mutual friend. Tall and slim, she had long dark blonde hair. She was shy, yet she had a dry pixie-like sense of humor. Most of the time she seemed to enjoy Chris's lively brothers. And they relished having a big sister to tease.

One night as we all, with the exception of Tim who was in Iowa City, rode in the car, we were singing *Wim-o-weh*, one of Susie's favorites. Jon and Ben relayed a plan to all of us except Susie to stop singing at a certain place in the song, allowing her to continue alone, which she did at the top of her lungs. The ruse worked perfectly and Susie, pretending (I think) humiliation, swore she would never forgive being tricked into a solo.

Chris, who eventually received a draft classification exempting him from service, first tried working as a carpenter. He concluded after a couple of job experiences that being a carpenter does not happen because you think it's a good idea to be a carpenter, took stock of his interests and abilities and decided to see what a career in physical therapy might be like. With good luck, he landed a job as a physical therapy aide in the local hospital.

In June of 1971 Chris and Susie were married under the care of the Ames Friends Meeting in a Quaker ceremony at the Boone County 4-H Camp near Boone, Iowa. We, by then residents of Kansas City, went back for the wedding. Susie's parents, brother and grandfather from Pittsburgh also were there.

It was a bright June day. The summer green of Iowa splashed about in the background surrounding the outdoor chapel, setting a pastoral scene. Family and friends, garb ranging from pure hippie to conventional and sedate, gathered on the rough-hewn backless benches and quietly waited for the couple to appear.

And then Chris and Susie, holding hands, appeared out of the woods and walked down the path. Such a handsome couple. They seemed fitted for one another — both tall, slim, lightly freckled, shy, smiling. Chris, wearing a navy blue blazer and blue summer pants, had cut his hair and beard. Gone was the wild and hairy hippie of some months before. Susie, a woman of simple but elegant tastes, wore a long muslin dress she had made herself. Her straight, dark blonde hair fell over her shoulders. They sat with the sponsoring couples, as meeting for worship began. Soon they rose, taking each other's hand. And turning toward one another, they repeated the traditional Quaker vows.

> "I, Christopher, take thee, Susan, to be my wife, promising to be unto thee a loving and faithful husband as long as we both shall live."
>
> "I, Susan, take thee, Christopher, to be my husband, promising to be unto thee a loving and faithful wife as long as we both shall live."

I breathed a prayer for their happiness. It all seemed so right.

Soon after the wedding, Chris and Susie (as we, his parents, had done so many years before) came out of a holding pattern and decided Chris needed to finish college and aim toward a career in physical therapy. So he went back to Iowa State University in November of 1971, working part-time as a physical therapy aide at Mary Greeley Hospital in Ames while he took a course of study leading to a degree in zoology which would make him eligible to apply for physical therapy school. Susie helped out with finances by working part-time in a bakery and doing other such odd jobs.

In June of 1974 Chris graduated. During those three years of school they seemed to get along together well. Chris worked hard and Susie, on their modest income, put together a pleasant and artistic home.

Chapter Five

CHRIS AND COLUMBIA — I

The Marriage

Chris and Susie moved to Columbia the summer of 1974. Before his graduation from Iowa State, he had applied to several physical therapy schools. They decided on the University of Missouri. The house they rented on a preliminary visit was within the city of Columbia, though Susie had wanted to live in the country. John, Tim, Jon and I drove from Kansas City to Columbia the day of their arrival to help them move in. For the first time, as they moved into the house, I sensed an unhappiness between them. However, I dismissed the questions in my mind; I knew moving was stressful.

It was good to have them closer. They came to Kansas City for holidays, and other times too. In a letter written to us in December 1988, Susie recalled: "... I remember how beautiful the shops and buildings (in Kansas City) were outlined in lights for Christmas, and I remember the flannel nightshirts I made for all the Griffith boys one year. I remember sitting at the table in your dining room, all of us gathered there together laughing and eating steaming mounds of food. I will never forget being a part of your family. ..."

Susie did adjust to living in town, and she got a job with

the university. Chris began a rigorous course in the school of physical therapy and held down a part-time job in the physical therapy department of the University of Missouri Medical Center. But before Chris graduated, Susie decided she wanted out of the marriage. It was a sorrowful time for Chris (for Susie too). Once he realized she was serious about ending the marriage, Chris let Susie go without making it more difficult for both of them than it was already.

Susie came to visit us in the days following her decision to leave Chris, hoping to make us understand that she didn't see a future for herself in their marriage. She didn't want us to feel we had done anything to hurt her nor did she want us to think she didn't care about Chris. To this day, I regret that I wasn't more friendly to her that day, for I, all of the family for that matter, truly loved Susie. That was part of what made it hard; the other part was that Chris was hurting. I remember his saying in a choked voice, "I thought Quaker marriages lasted forever."

In the spring of 1976, Chris finished physical therapy school with a G.P.A. of 3.77. John and I went to the graduation dinner given for the physical therapy students; it was evident that Chris, one of the oldest students in the class, was popular with his classmates. We had come prepared to spend the night and go to graduation the next day. When we mentioned this, Chris laughed and assured us we could go to the graduation if we wished, but he didn't plan to be there. While finishing the course was important, the graduation ceremony had little meaning for him. So we spent the night in Columbia as we had planned and the next morning took him to breakfast at Howard Johnson's.

His next step was a year's internship at the University Hospital in Charleston, South Carolina. There, in the state where his father had been born and raised, away from Columbia, he spent what seemed to us to be a healing year. He made friends, including some of the black employees at the hospital; he told of feeling especially honored to be invited to visit a black country church with his newfound friends. He reveled in the black gospel music and apparently rose to the occasion of being asked, as a special honor, to pass the collection plate.

Although the dissolution of his marriage was painful to him, he wasn't bitter toward Susie. Even after she remarried, he continued to keep in touch with her and visited Susie and her husband in their home several times.

The Physical Therapist

Chris's career as a physical therapist began at Rusk Rehabilitation Center in Columbia, Mo., in June 1977; his first stint at Rusk continued until June 1982. His work in physical therapy in those years included work with those who had had strokes, people with head injuries, persons who were disabled from accidents or disease and who were trying to move from wheel chairs to more inclusive lives — children and adults — the whole gamut of physical therapy work.

It seemed to us he felt his work was worthwhile. At the beginning of 1982, however, he became involved in working for peace and began to entertain notions of quitting work for a while to do full-time peace work. In addition to that, he had begun to wonder (in Chris-like fashion) whether he might find a facet of physical therapy in which he would feel as if he were making more of a difference to the total person. After debating for several months what to do, he finally decided to take a break to organize his life and work in peace activities (more about this later). As was typical of Chris, he had enough money saved to last him a year if he decided that was what he wanted to do.

However, he didn't stay away from his profession for more than a few months. According to his friend Bill, professional people kept asking him when he was coming back to work and he finally decided — the adventure of non-employment had about run its course — to accept one of the options offered him, a job as a physical therapist on a team of persons in

Columbia Public Schools who were to prepare children with disabilities to enter public schools. It was not as remunerative as some physical therapy jobs, but the idea of working with children appealed to him. He stayed in this position from February 1983 until the spring of 1986.

He found special satisfaction in his work with children. Their disabilities covered physical and emotional problems — autism, Down's syndrome, accidents — anything which would interfere with a child starting to public school. Each child was treated as an individual; in Chris's files were carefully worked out exercises for his children. He was well-loved by the children and by those with whom he worked.

> Chris has been an integral part of the success of our programs for young children. I will not forget observing Chris during our preschool screening. You

Chris congratulates a patient at Rusk Rehabilitation Center, Columbia, MO.

could hear him say "Good jumping, John" or "Way to go, Sam." All the children felt very comfortable when working with Chris because of his warmth and care toward them. We do miss Chris.

— Lynn Barnett, Special Education Director,
Columbia Public Schools, October 27, 1986

By the spring of 1986, when his contract came up for renewal, it had become clear to him that he would like to get into a physical therapy job that would move him toward a specialty. So a few months before his death, he went back to Rusk where he began work in a new and innovative preventive back care program. In a letter August 6, 1986, to his friend and former roommate, John Markovitz, he said, "I like my new job, and it is demanding a great deal from me. We will see how I like it in a year. . . ."

Not long before his death he had begun to consider going back to school part-time to get a graduate degree in counseling with a thought of eventually getting into private practice as a physical therapist who would also be able to counsel patients. It seemed a good idea to us.

As his parents, we feel that Chris, most of the time anyway, was comfortable as a physical therapist. Parents sometimes don't know what sons and daughters really think and feel; we do believe, though, that Chris was honest with us when he claimed basic satisfaction with his profession.

As a professional person, his former supervisors can attest that he did go through times of being stubborn about his appearance — he had the notion that how he dressed and whether he had a beard, scruffy or well-trimmed, was not of great importance. However, he and his supervisors and cohorts at work weathered those times; I suspect there was compromise on both sides. To the best of our knowledge, there was never serious question as to his capability as a physical therapist. And his qualifications as a caring human being seemed never to have been in question.

Upon his death we heard from patients, parents of children enrolled in the public schools program, classmates in physical therapy, staff members at both Rusk and the schools program.

> I was a patient of Chris at Rusk . . . I just want Chris's family to know how wonderful I thought he was and I will never forget knowing him. . . .
>
> — Patient from Belle, MO, September 30, 1986

> . . . it is ten years since I last saw him. Despite this I remember Chris with much fondness. I recall his compassion with his patients and his classmates; and he always had a kind or encouraging word for anyone he met. . . .
>
> — physical therapy classmate, October 19, 1986

> . . . My son Chris attended Parkade ECLC program about two years ago. I just wanted to tell you how much your son Chris did for our son Chris. He was the most caring person in that program and also one of the most caring people I have ever met. . . . My Chris loved your Chris so much — even though he couldn't say it with words, you could see it in the hugs and kisses he gave your Chris. . . .
>
> — Mother of an autistic child, December 11, 1986

> . . . We knew him to be a kind and gentle person, and an excellent physical therapist who was committed to the welfare of his patients. . . .
>
> — Susan S. Deusinger, M.A., P.T.,
> Missouri Physical Therapy Assn., Oct. 14, 1986

When there has been a death, we know people, in an effort to soothe the pain, sometimes overpraise. In Chris's case, we choose to hold onto belief in the sincerity we felt behind the kind words of those who wrote and spoke to us of him.

Besides, the experiences they relate fit with what we knew of Chris as a son.

Chapter Six

CHRIS AND COLUMBIA — II

Back in the seventies other changes began,
Some women started to show their hands,
They said, "We don't need no man,
Women, let's do what we can."

Now it's the eighties, it's the same old thing,
Men can be drafted to die again,
So come on men, now form a ring,
They can't make an army of lovin' men.

from *Back in the Sixties*
a song by Chris Griffith

This part of the story of Chris and Columbia begins in 1978 and is devoted to Chris and the man he became outside his professional life.

Home, Sweet Home

Chris could never quite decide whether to live in town or in the country. When he was in town, he liked the convenience of city life, often riding his bicycle to work. On the other hand, he yearned to be in a quiet place with natural surroundings. The countryside around Columbia is hilly and wooded; small, clear streams nestle between wooded hills. For someone imbued with a Daniel Boone spirit, it is a tempting place to live in spite of inconvenience. So Chris moved about, trying to balance love of the woods, economy, being near friends, privacy, and the inclinations of the current roommate or roommates.

John Markovitz probably spent more time as Chris's roommate than anyone else. John, with some scratching of head, chronicled the story of their moves.

They first met through mutual friends in 1978 soon after John came to Columbia. Chris, who had been back from South Carolina for several months, lived with a young man named Rob in a place in the country he referred to as "Fox Hollow." I remember it as a rundown place way back in the woods over several bridges and lots of hills. There were some goats, maybe other animals, which belonged to the owner, on the place. We have pictures of Chris with the goats; I am told the goats sometimes followed him on his ramblings about the countryside. The house, heated with wood, was livable, though a bit airy in the winter.

"From the first, I was drawn to Chris," John says. He sometimes visited Chris in Fox Hollow where they would talk and play music. Also, Chris was a physical therapist, and John was going to school in the hope he would eventually be able to get into physical therapy school himself.

When Chris decided to move from Fox Hollow, he, John and a friend, Steve Call, rented a cheap house in a rough neighborhood in Columbia where they lived for a year. (I believe that was the house Chris encouraged us not to visit.) They decided to move from there after John got beaten up by a group of young kids in an attempted robbery. There was an amusing aspect to this attack, serious as it might have been. When one of the attackers kicked John in the leg, the leg fell off. John, an amputee, had a prosthetic leg. The mob stared in amazement and then scattered.

The next neighborhood was a safer one. John, Chris and Steve moved there together. John tells how Chris had problems with Steve's laid-back attitude toward housekeeping responsibilities (it's difficult to see how Chris, himself no paragon of neatness, could have had such problems). Chris was most irritated because Steve regularly forgot to put the mustard in the refrigerator. John emphasized that Chris was very patient, urging Steve gently to please put the mustard away in the refrigerator, with very uneven results. One day as Chris and John were in the kitchen eating, John asked Chris if he wanted any mustard on his sandwich. With a resigned sigh, Chris said, "No, I think it's rotten."

A couple of years later Chris and John moved to a quite presentable brick house on Glenwood where they inherited two roommates, Dexter and Wendy. Dexter, who was working on a doctorate in a scientific field (I forget which), occupied the basement suite. Wendy, also in school, managed to hold her own quite well with the three young men in the house. Not the Wendy of Peter Pan, she would not be imposed upon for "womanly" chores.

John was taking courses preparatory to application to physical therapy school. As the time drew near for him to complete his work, Chris, in a heart-to-heart talk, cautioned him not to be disappointed if he should be rejected; Chris was afraid his grades weren't high enough.

Well, John was rejected. At this point Chris, in an offhand way, asked, "John, have you ever thought of nursing?" At first John was miffed that Chris seemed to dismiss his chances of getting into physical therapy and at the proper interval, reapplied. In the meantime, he had read of a nursing school in St. Louis that caught his fancy. When the second rejection came, he was already accepted in St. Louis. So he packed up and moved there to go to nursing school, grateful that he had listened to Chris out of one corner of his mind.

Chris stayed on at the Glenwood house with Wendy and Dexter. When John came back from St. Louis, he rented an acreage in the country he had always admired on Rock Quarry Road. The house, small and old, was located at the top of a hill on a grassy spot with woods down the hill and all around. Not far from town, it was accessible, and while not as remote as Fox Hollow, it was an oasis of quiet. Chris, apparently antsy to be in the country again, moved in with John. They lived there together until John decided to try his nursing skills in the backwoods of Kentucky. So he packed his things into a U-Haul, told Chris good-bye, and drove away.

"That was the last time I saw Chris," John said with sadness. Chris stayed on in the house alone until his death. Indecisive and careful as usual, Chris was in the midst of the laborious process of weighing whether or not he should buy some property. And if so, where — country or town?

Personal Growth

As Chris's parents, we look back on his later years in Columbia as a time of personal growth. We are aware there were times of agonizing personal decisions. Yet there were deep and satisfying friendships, active interests and involvement in good causes, full and happy times. Most of all, we felt he grew as he mulled over the pieces of his life in his own mind and in conversation with good friends and family. Chris was not one to exist in a static environment; he was open to change and new ways of thinking. And it seemed important to him that his life have meaning, not only for his own happiness but also for the welfare of others — an ongoing dilemma for him.

One friend, Suzy Morse, wrote of that time, "He struggled with so many issues — never seeming to give himself a break — reaching deep into his soul, thrashing things out about relationships between people, specifically men and women, men and men, friendship, love escaping the narrow roles society presented. He seemed to go beyond the first level of that exploration, beyond sexism defined as just being oppressive to women. . . ."

With causes, we observed that his involvement was not casual. He didn't take part in organizations just to be doing something to feel good about himself; he measured what he was doing. If by his own standards, he felt he was not contributing to the cause the organization represented, he moved on to something else. But while he was involved, he expended his share, sometimes more than his share, of energy, time and caring.

Suzy confirms this impression, ". . . he was always questioning the value of things and being self-critical, always searching for a direction that would seem a clear calling with no hesitations — and I'm not sure he ever found that . . . But while all this was going on inside he did commit great amounts of ongoing time and energy to his project over the long haul."

The Co-op Grocery Store. Chris had from childhood, as noted before, an attachment for food, and he liked grocery stores. One of our early visits to Columbia, soon after he and Susie had moved there, was memorable for a tour of a grocery Chris particularly liked. I remember Susie being embarrassed by Chris's eagerness to show us the store. "Oh Chris," she said, "for heavens sakes, they don't want to see a grocery store." But Chris serenely showed us the store with its huge variety of fruits and vegetables, his favorite foods.

The food co-op began in the mid-seventies with a group of back-to-nature people who wanted a place to buy good, cheap, organic health foods. In 1978, it moved to a storefront, and as it grew to include more people, the inevitable happened — factions formed. Two main groups squared off — those who wished to maintain a vegetarian/health food store and those who wanted a co-op membership grocery store with many of the products found in "regular" groceries.

It was natural that Chris, raised on the cooperative philosophy and interested in good food, became active in the co-op almost from the first, both as a worker and in the politics of the organization. And since he listened to people who expressed their needs, he took the questions posed by others in the membership seriously. On more than one visit home, I can remember that he grieved over problems between people in the co-op. As the controversy heated up, Chris at one point was asked to be a mediator because it was thought he would be fair, a real compliment. I don't know whether he performed this task or not; if he did, I'm sure he didn't take it lightly! His friend, Bill Clark, says, "Chris started out as a co-op purist and grew to have a more practical viewpoint."

His interest in the co-op continued up until his death, although in the last couple years we didn't hear as much about the politics.

Peace. After his death, several of Chris's friends mentioned a photo of Chris, resplendent in full beard and lots of hair, dancing in the aisle of a school bus, a wild and happy grin on his face. We found it among his things. It was taken in June of 1982 on a trip to the national FREEZE rally in Washington. Chris had obtained a chauffeur's license especially for the occasion so that he could help drive the bus the local FREEZE group used to travel to the rally.

As mentioned earlier, one of reasons for quitting his physical therapy work in 1982 for a few months was to work for peace, and the trip to Washington was part of the life of Chris, the peace activist. During that summer, he helped set up the nuclear FREEZE office in Columbia, circulated petitions and helped facilitate meetings. Other peace work during the early 1980s included help in the organization of Oxfam fasts, one way to empathize with the many hungry people in the world.

We believe that although these activities were important

to Chris, he found his freewheeling spirit sometimes didn't fit the constraints of already functioning organizations as well as the more informal interests he developed. Some of his experiences with these activities are recounted below.

But first, interweaving with the activities was an interest in music. Through music he was able to express some of his deepest feelings.

Music. They would sit down together, the two tallest of our sons, their heads, auburn and dark brown, bent over Chris's guitar, and Ben, the youngest, would try to teach what he knew to his big brother. In response to a rekindled interest in music, Chris had purchased a guitar sometime during the early years after Susie's departure. And although he was endowed with a good singing voice, he did not have an instinctual gift for rhythm and chords. He had to learn how to play the guitar. In the first year after Chris bought his guitar, Ben, the musician brother who lives in Kentucky, gave Chris guitar lessons during the few times he saw him.

Later, Chris decided he needed weekly instruction and for several years took lessons from a friend in Columbia. He learned to play well enough to accompany himself, sometimes others. As he had in other efforts, Chris worked hard at learning to play the guitar. Then he started to write his own songs. They usually centered around issues he was concerned with at the time.

"Hey, this is a song I wrote," he would say to us on his visits home as he sat on the couch with his guitar. And we would listen and say, "That's nice, Chris," or "Good work," or "I like the beat," or something else offhand. If only we could hear him sing his songs now — we didn't realize then how much his songs were a part of him.

At the time of his death, we discovered among his things a tape which was recorded in November of 1984. I can remember the first time we listened to the tape a few days after his death. The pain of hearing his rich, strong voice with the knowledge that we would not see him again was almost more than we could bear. However, as the words sank through the pain, we made a discovery of infinite importance to us; his songs revealed much about the probing, caring nature of our eldest son. Some of the words from these songs are included in this chapter and throughout the book.

Men's (and Women's) Issues. BRAVO (Brothers Resolved Against Violence and Oppression), formed in 1982, was an organization which combined Chris's interest in men's issues and his concerns about violence. He was on the board of BRAVO at the time of his death.

In response to the stirring of feminism in the 1970s, men's groups began to appear over the country in the late 1970s and 1980s. Chris was involved in a men's group in Columbia which began around 1980. Splintering off was another group concerned about the issues of domestic violence. Two interests were uppermost in this group which met together in 1981–82: (1) men's relationships to domestic violence; (2) rape prevention. The group spawned two organizations: (1) BRAVO (Brothers Resolved Against Violence and Oppression), (2) RPEP (Rape Prevention Education Project).

BRAVO was concerned with men who felt violence was a problem in their relationships with women and families. One of the men on the forming group was a counselor who was aware of men who needed help with this problem. So the BRAVO group started a support group for men who wanted to meet together to discuss their own problems with violence in the home. Agencies and individuals made referrals to this group. Chris helped conduct these meetings.

There also was an umbrella organization formed for BRAVO and RPEP — Mid-Missouri Men's Resource Group (MMRG); until his death Chris was treasurer of that group.

We understand BRAVO still meets weekly in a room at a

counseling agency in Columbia. Chris's friend and former roommate, John Markovitz, who became a facilitator for BRAVO after Chris's death, reported in mid-1991 that the number of court-referred men has increased. Formerly most of the men were self-referred. This has resulted in a more structured approach. John also said two graduates of BRAVO are taking leadership roles in the organization.

BRAVO and MMRG were dear to Chris's heart. The discussions he had with other men seemed to reach some of the questions he had about relationships of men and women, women and women, and men and men.

Guiniveres are kissed by mothers kind,
While they're babies young,
Fathers don't kiss Lancelots at all,
Only words of strength are sung.

Chorus:
It's all a part of the crazy game,
It's all a part of the lie, the lie,
It's all a part of the sad, sad game,
That you, my brother, must die, must die,
That you, my brother, must die.

from *Camelot*
a song by Chris Griffith

A Star Is Born. Another spin-off of Chris's concern for men's issues was the production of a series of radio programs. The first of these, *Men Freeing Men,* was done in partnership with his friend, Francis Baumli. The show began in late February of 1982 and was broadcast over the Public Community Radio Station KOPN once a month for two hours.

Francis writes, "It was oriented toward men's liberation and combatting sexism against both men and women. The title of the first show, aired Feb. 28, 1982, was "Men and War: The

Quest for Peace." Other representative shows were: "Men Having Fun," "The National Coalition of Free Men," "The Rights of Single Male Parents," and "Sexism in Music."

A year after its start, Chris decided the radio show was taking too much time. Francis continued to produce the show by himself until July of 1983.

However, it appeared that Chris could not quite give up the idea of radio for he got involved some time later with three friends — Olaf Kula, Forrest McGill and Bill Clark — in another program entitled "Good-bye John Wayne" (the title of the show is based on a song by Geoff Morgan). This program was designed to help men reevaluate their roles in society. The changing role of fathers, friendship of men with each other, friendship of straight men with gay men, childhood experiences and the effect of sports on men were some of the issues addressed by this program. It was produced for two years. The song below reflects some of his thinking on these issues.

Chorus:
How can I write a song
When the words don't seem to rhyme,
How can I sing a song
When the rhythm beats out of time.

Verse 2
I've been taught the words to songs
Of a bold and ferocious kind,
I've been taught the rhythms hard
Of the gun, the drum, the fife.

I've been taught the song of love
Between a man and his loving wife,
But the words don't always rhyme
And the rhythm beats out of time.

I've been taught to sing my songs
To those women I hold so dear,
But in songs to men I love,
The words and rhymes aren't clear.

from *How Can I Write a Song*
a song by Chris Griffith

Folk Dancing. A friend recalls: "I met Chris along with a whole group of folk dancers on May Day at a folk dance out in an idyllic country setting. A maypole was up in a clearing in the woods. People rode by on horseback. . . . The group did Irish and old American contradances, often to live music. When the 'teacher' left for Kansas City and the future of the group was in doubt, Chris took over the responsibility, and as I remember it, basically made it possible for the group to continue. . . . This went on for some time, then others began to learn how to call and shared the responsibility and eventually he went back to being a participant."

Last year I found a clipping, apparently sent to us by Chris, of a story (no date) from *The Missourian,* the university paper. The story was written by Elizabeth Simpson, a staff writer. There is a photo of a group of people folk dancing; Chris is in the foreground. The writer tells of going to a university mall to observe live music and folk dancing with the idea of doing a feature on a folk dancing group that met each Monday evening in a university quadrangle during nice weather (moving during cold weather into a university building). Chris, apparently the caller that night, insisted she dance rather than watch. In spite of panic concerning her abilities, she got caught up in the dancing and "swung around as gracefully as a board, laughed, clapped and sang until nightfall."

At that point, Chris asked, "Coming back next week?"

"Wouldn't miss it," she answered.

"Great. Reporter turns dancer," was his reply.

I don't know how long Chris was involved in the folk dancing group; it was obvious from the enthusiasm with which he spoke of this activity that he enjoyed it very much.

Chorus: (folk dance beat)
Allemand left with the old left hand,
Round the ring with a right and left grand,
Round the ring with a gee and a haw,
Swing that gal from Arkansas.

Step right back and give her a grin,
Step right up and swing again,
Step right back and give her a smile,
Step right up and swing awhile.

Verse 4:
The sweat runs down over our brows,
It's fun to move while the fiddle sounds,
We keep on stepping, our shoes wear thin,
The music fills our souls within.

Sometimes I wonder where we'll go,
Hope God has a fiddle and bow,
So I can dance on clouds of white,
And dance with every angel in sight.

from *The Folk Dance*
a song by Chris Griffith

And when the earth shall claim your limbs, then shall you truly dance.

— from *The Prophet* by Kahlil Gibran

Nature. The card reads, "CERTIFIED RIVER RAT. This certifies that the bearer, Christopher Griffith, is a qualified member of the Missouri River Rat Association, and has met the membership criteria as listed on the back of this card." Criteria include: "at some time have been immersed in a

Missouri float stream; have capsized a canoe not deliberately; have, on occasion, taken the more adventuresome fork in the river; have always camped and canoed in such a way as to have shown concern for the environment." A very suitable mix for Chris.

Missouri rivers in the central and southern parts of the state are ideal for the average canoe enthusiast — clear, scenic, normally not too fast, though the more adventuresome can experience mild thrills. Chris spent many happy hours on the water with friends: in the spring, enjoying the fresh green of a world waking from the chill of winter; in the summer, soaking up the sun's rays on a lazy float trip; in the fall, absorbing the beauty from the splashes of color around every bend of the river.

Chris was pretty hung-up on the environment. He carried a quiet anger at what is happening to the natural beauty of our earth.

Chorus:
Mother Earth she calls you,
She calls you by your name,
Mother Earth she calls you,
Don't you hear her sad refrain?
Children, don't stab me,
Stab me with your knife,
Children, don't stab me
And take my sweet, sweet life;
Children don't squeeze me
By my pretty throat,
Children don't squeeze me,
Hear those words I spoke;
Put your head to the ground
And hear the earth's sound,
Put your head to the ground
And hear the earth's sound.

from *The Sweet Earth*
a song by Chris Griffith

Suzy Morse recalls, "We were so bedraggled that while we waited for you to pick us up, a well-meaning family came along and spontaneously offered us money." She and Chris had taken a backpacking trip to Colorado, going by bus, hiking in the Rockies where they experienced the vast beauty and grandeur of the West and close-up views of tiny mountain flowers and moss, hitchhiking in the rain because of bus strikes, arriving back in Kansas City soaked to the skin.

Backpacking was another pleasure which for Chris combined exercise and seeing nature at a slow pace. John Markovitz and Chris took a trip West together six or seven years before Chris's death in John's old VW squareback packed with camping gear, bicycles secured to the outside, an unbelievable sight. Somehow Chris managed to fold his long body into the front seat. At one point, they were camped somewhere and the car wouldn't start. While John raved and pounded the car, Chris disappeared and returned soon with a man with tools who fixed the car and wouldn't take any money. Among Chris's talents, was the ability to strike up useful conversation.

That trip was taken in May; at the edge of Yellowstone Park they found a river with hot springs where they swam. In the Tetons it was cold, so somehow they curled up and slept in the car. Their final plan, to ride their bikes around a lake north of Missoula (a trip of several days) was aborted in one day because of a steady, cold rain.

On the way home they spent a night with a friend of John's in Boulder where John, for the day they were there, struck up a short romance with the roommate of his friend. As they drove back to Columbia, John tells that Chris confided that it really made him angry that John was able to do that sort of thing. For Chris, relationships were deliberated upon and agonized over, not instantaneous. Chris liked the lightness with which John moved among people; John was in awe of the intensity Chris put into his relationships. John says, "I guess that's one reason Chris and I had such a wonderful friendship — because we admired different aspects of one another."

Chris took other trips West. In a small diary of the last trip he took West in the summer of 1984 when he helped a friend, a young single mother, Teresa Graham, and her son, Dylan, move West, he notes, "I saw two eagles and a wren yesterday, along with various other birds. Golly, the world is wonderful."

> *Verse 1:*
> There's hope all around us
> Like strawberries on a hill,
> So gather round good people,
> We've got a message to tell.
>
> *Chorus:*
> We've got sunshine on our shoulders,
> We've got moonbeams in our hands,
> Spring provides us lift-off,
> And winter a strong tail wind.
>
> from *Montana Serenade*
> a song by Chris Griffith

Chris also loved to hike, one of the attractions of living in the country. At the time of his death, his favorite place to hike around Columbia was the Gans Creek area. A friend writes, "He found much peace and delight there — and I still feel his presence there strongly, especially in the calls of the hoot owls and mourning doves."

We sometimes think of the time he took us to his favorite spot above Gans Creek. We had walked and walked and then as we came to the cliff overlooking the creek, with a triumphant smile, he thrust his long arms out for us to behold the sight. It was as if he were sharing a wonderful secret with us.

Chapter Seven

CHRIS AND COLUMBIA — III

A friend is an easy thing to be,
It's easy to laugh, don't you see,
Yes, it's a friend I wanna be,
Babe, won't you please be friends with me?
from *Friends, Lovers and Strangers*
a song by Chris Griffith

Chris and People

Although Chris had always had friends, he was not a gregarious person. In the years in Columbia, it seemed as if his time had come to have friends and to be a friend. He is remembered as a caring person who gave much to his friends and family including time, counsel, even timely loans.

His friend, Francis Baumli, wrote, "Defining adult interactions with his brothers, and his parents, was a big struggle for Chris. He wanted all of them — himself, brothers, and parents — to feel like 'equals.' He no longer wanted to work in terms of sibling dynamics, nor did he want to feel, when he was interacting with his parents, as though there was a child/parent relationship.

"Happily for him, he felt that he was making much progress toward what he wanted on this before he died. The last night I spent with Chris, August 27, 1986, we went to see the movie, *Stand by Me*. After the movie, we were going to go to a bar or lounge, but it seemed every place we might have visited was closed that night. At one point I said, 'This is silly. We don't need to sit in a bar and talk. Let's just go to where my car is, and sit in the car and talk.' Which we did, for maybe an hour and a half. During that conversation, Chris talked at length about how he had been to visit his parents recently, and told them things about himself which he had never before divulged, and that he felt he was moving toward the kind of adult-to-adult relationship he wanted."

We concur with Francis on this observation, for we remember the occasion of that visit with Chris in which we felt like privileged friends sharing a special confidence. We could sense it was important to him to be able to feel our love extend to him beyond our being his parents. In fact, our relationship with Chris had become one of deep and loving friendship. Since he often visited us by himself, we found ourselves in the last two or three years of his life doing things together like three good friends.

John and I will never forget Chris's leave-taking the last time he was home. As he departed, the three of us stood in a circle in the middle of the living room and shared a gigantic hug. That is our last memory of being with him, our last physical contact with this son/friend.

And while he was working with family relationships, he was also, as mentioned before, working on relationships with his friends. One of his songs is especially concerned with this aspect of his life; it is a plea to be ourselves with one another.

Verses 1 and 2:
I wanna run naked and dance with the sun,
I wanna run naked and love everyone,
I wanna run naked so I might be
Just my, just my loving me.

I wanna run naked and cry with the rain,
I wanna run naked, start my life again,
I wanna run naked and shout to the sky,
I wanna wave that other life goodbye.

from *I Wanna Run Naked*
a song by Chris Griffith

Bill Clark, in a letter written in December after Chris's death, tells "just a sweet story." Bill and Chris sometimes played pool together Friday evenings. "Chris brought out my less competitive side," he wrote, "but I also was prone to disturbing his apple cart sometimes because he provided me with such wonderful responses.

"One evening he brought his intended shot right to the brink of the corner pocket, but not in. As I pondered my shot I had to be careful not to bump the table as it seemed his ball might yet fall in. I had no good easy shot. . . .

"So in a mischievous moment I decided to try one of those trick shots that professionals do to cruelly prevent their opponent from having an advantage. I bumped his ball so that it rolled out away from the pocket. Chris, thinking I had done it accidentally, said, with a concerned look on his face, 'Bill, you're shooting at the wrong balls!' I said, 'No, I'm just preventing your shot.' It turned out very unsatisfying for me, because slowly a look came over his face that resembled that of a child who had just been told that there is no Santa Claus. He was truly shocked to find that his buddy Bill would stoop to being ruthless. Then, I suspect, just to prove that good overcomes evil, he proceeded to beat me."

While Bill makes himself the bad guy in the preceding story, the relationship between Bill and Chris was, as the story illustrates, a close one. (They even looked alike — both tall and almost red-headed.) In another letter to us, Bill wrote, "Chris and I spoke often of our thrill about the miracle of childbirth. We once promised that if we each got married, the first one of us to have a child would do our best to include the other in the birth experience." Bill and Marta were married in the second year after Chris's death. At their wedding, "We held a moment of silence for joyful remembrance of Christopher and many people thanked us, saying memory of him was strong on that day. Thanks once again for having had that boy who so enriched my life." (In June of 1992 Bill and Marta adopted a most satisfactory baby boy.)

Another marriage of friends of Chris, Teresa Sweeney and Steve Call, (his former roommate) took place September 26, 1987 out on the land where Chris last lived and where friends of his had lived prior to his time there and where more friends lived at the time of the wedding. Teresa wrote, "People spoke of Chris and of the slow healing that they were undergoing and of the hope that was generated by our being there together at a happy time. Some felt that Chris's joy and laughter and music were there, part of our ceremony. In our wedding we remembered Chris by our vows which expressed our 'faith not only in the endurance of people, but also in their generosity, grace and love.' He is still alive for us in an empowering, spirited way."

Dylan. Two of Chris's friends spoke of his relationship with Dylan, mentioned earlier. (Dylan was the son of Chris's friend, Teresa Graham, a single mother.) For the month of August 1982, when Dylan was five, Chris cared for Dylan at his house while Teresa, who was in nursing school, struggled through summer school.

In a letter written at that time to a friend, Chris said, "It is wonderful to be greeted by his smiling face in the morning and to snuggle down with him and read a book. It is fun to see him relate with his environment. . . ."

Another friend, remembering that extended visit, told the story of Dylan and his introduction to the world of sweets. Teresa had raised Dylan as a country boy (in Arkansas) and kept his diet healthful. Chris tried to maintain the same kind of supervision. However, he could not control the neighbors who found Dylan charming. (This was at the time Chris lived in the house on Glenwood with Wendy and Dexter.) It was especially hard to control Dylan's whereabouts on Saturday mornings. One Saturday Chris woke up to find Dylan gone from the bed he had fixed for him in his room.

"Have you seen Dylan?" he asked Wendy, as he strode into the kitchen, looking worried.

Wendy laughed and reminded him it was Saturday morning and Dylan was out in the neighborhood "cruising for sweets." Chris found him, confiscated the goodies, fed him a good breakfast, holding the sweets hostage until later.

We remember when Dylan stayed with Chris that time. It was a special time for the bachelor to deal with this young child. Chris often mentioned how he hoped there would be a time in his life when he would have a child of his own. This was the closest he got to that dream. I often wonder what a child of Christopher's would have been like. Probably tall with dark brown eyes, auburn hair and a smattering of freckles on his nose!

Dylan's mom, Teresa, says of Chris, ". . . without having known Christopher the scars of my past experiences would have wounded me for life. Just the fact that such a person existed was healing. . . . He helped us in many ways that were much more subtle and too many ways to even mention. I loved him very much as did my son, Dylan. . . ."

Women in His Life. Yes, there were women in Chris's life. In fact, we were introduced to some very nice women friends of Christopher's in the years after his divorce. We don't know how close he came to marriage with any of these good women friends. We do know that he tended to take relationships with women seriously. Breaking up with a woman was hard for him and he agonized, sometimes even to his parents, when a relationship ended. The pain of his divorce seemed to make him cautious; it was as if he were afraid to risk the closeness and possible pain of a broken marriage again.

These wonderful unnamed women — they know who they are — added warmth and love to Chris's life. We are grateful. We deeply regret he could not have lived long enough for another happy marriage experience, perhaps with children.

Other Friends Speak

"The times that I shared with Chris, seeing him in the school where my daughter spends her days, singing with him in our kitchen, stopping to chat whenever we met, all helped me to remember that I too can find the smile in my heart, can have courage when faced with difficult challenges, can listen and cry with friends over the tragedies that shock us, and truly hurt.

"Chris, the spiritual man, most likely still dreams the same dream, of a world at peace, and of people at peace with themselves. I am confident that he believed in that dream because his whole life supported it. And because he dreamed it, believed it, lived it, others have found ways to make it true, at least in their own lives here in Columbia and, I am sure, beyond here."

These two touching and eloquent paragraphs are the words of a young woman, a reformed alcoholic, who wrote them in a letter to us a few days after Chris's death.

Chris could not be characterized as a do-gooder. He didn't seem intentionally to strive to strike up helping relationships. Yet in the course of his daily life, his friends included persons in need of special aid. It was obvious that it gave him pleasure to help his friends.

Among these was Bruce LaFleur, a young man with cerebral palsy who used a wheel chair. Chris and Bruce became such good friends that Chris built or had built a ramp at the Glenwood house so that Bruce (and others) could have access to the house. Although their initial introduction took place through Friends Meeting (Chris was an off-and-on attender there), not on a professional level, Chris's interest in Bruce and his welfare led him to enlist professional help for Bruce.

In his work, Chris not only dealt with the problems of his patients, he also, through his music, articulated some of the pain. One of his songs is about persons paralyzed with lower back injuries.

Hey babe
I am a man
Who ain't got hands
That can reach up high
And touch that smile.
. . .
Why me babe?
Why I'm so young
To be among
The lonely crowd
And not be sound.
. . .
Tears, pains, laughs, games,
Visions rise and alone he lies,
Tales of woe always flow
A dying bird told me so.

from *Reflections*
a song by Chris Griffith

And he was concerned with more than just the ramifications of physical injury. He was aware that many (probably most) of us have some limitation to overcome.

Chorus:
You've gotta grab your hat
And reach for your star,
You're the only one who

Knows what you are,
Like a lion with a cub
You've gotta nurture with love,
Like a wolf after prey
You've gotta hunt night and day,
Like a deer on the run
With an arrow in its thigh
You've gotta work, work hard,
Or fall down and die,
It's true, I know it, I feel it in my bones,
It's true, I know it, I feel it in my soul,
It's true, I know it, you gotta see what's whole.
See what's whole.

from *You Gotta Grab Your Hat*
a song by Chris Griffith

In writing of Chris and Columbia, I have mentioned only a few of Chris's Columbia friends whose lives mingled with his. For those friends who have not been named here, we want you to know it is not because you aren't equally valued. Your names and faces are stored in our memories. You have spoken in person and by letter with us many times in the years since his death. Through the invisible cord of friendship and caring, we have heard your voices and felt the warmth of your hands on ours. You are in our hearts for us as long as we live.

One of our unkept promises to Chris was to come visit him soon. He wanted us to spend time with him and his friends. It is our loss that we had not kept this promise. However, through the sad circumstance of his death we have now spent time with his friends. For his friends have become our friends as they have demonstrated their love for this very special man.

Chapter Eight

I see, see, oh I see,
Beyond that indigo tree,
As she flies away from me
That vision will keep me free.
When I die, oh I die,
My soul will always fly,
With that lovely indigo bird,
While the meadowlark's song is heard.

from *Indigo Bunting Morning*
a song by Chris Griffith

Saturday, September 13, the day of the memorial service, arrived.

All of the family at our house drove to Columbia that morning. We carried a lunch packed by sister-in-law Ann to eat at Chris's house before the service. Forrest, Bill, Penny and other friends of Chris's greeted us there. They had cleaned up the house for our coming (affectionately aware that Chris's housekeeping skills were minimal).

We ate lunch on Chris's picnic table under the shade of some large old trees in the yard. As we sat there together, a light breeze stirred the leaves on the tree above the table. We talked of Chris, trying to keep our conversation light. We asked Penny if she would like to have the picnic table and she said she would. Would Bill want the water bed? Well, yes, if we didn't. I remember saying through tears, "I keep thinking we should know who has his things because he'll be coming back. I know better, but I don't want to..." And Penny put her arm around me.

The memorial service, held in a large room at an ecumenical student center adjacent to the First Presbyterian Church, was a time of quiet dedication to Chris's memory.

> FRIENDS SHARE SORROW, ANGER
>
> During an hour-long memorial service Saturday, those who knew Chris Griffith shared their grief and their memories. The 38-year-old University physical therapist, was one of the four people murdered Tuesday while in a wildlife area in Marshall, MO. ...
>
> The first few minutes of the 2:00 P.M. service were devoted to silence, which was broken only by mourners' sobs and sniffles.
>
> Then in the Quaker tradition, mourners shared the sorrow and anger of their loss, speaking to the group as their emotions moved them. And they shared their memories ...
>
> As the service ended, everyone in the room joined hands and observed a few final minutes of silence for their lost friend, brother and son. "Those who die live on in the hearts and minds of people who are still here. I know he will for me," said Susan Sweetland. (Chris's friend and former supervisor in the public schools program.)
>
> — *The Missourian*, September 14, 1986

Over two hundred persons — friends, patients, family members, and others — were there. We were touched that Susie, Chris's former wife, and her husband drove from Tuscaloosa, Alabama to attend the service. A friend of ours from Kansas City, up until then an admired acquaintance, now a treasured friend, came "for you." Other family and friends from a distance came for us and for Chris.

The service was based on the Quaker custom of silent worship; anyone who wished to do so was free to speak out of the silence. The only planned words were the obituary and the poem that came to me as we made our nighttime drive to Kansas City in the early morning hours of September 10.

TO CHRIS

"This is my beloved son, in whom I am well pleased."

I am pleased with your compassion and your gentleness;
with the love in your heart;

I am pleased with your tall, erect body;
with your mass of auburn hair
and your soft, full voice;

I am pleased with your caring spirit;
with your solemn search for truth;

I am pleased that you have lived to become more than a
child to your father and me . . .
dear and loving friend.

I shall love the memory of you
and miss you all the days of my life.

— Reva Griffith, September 10, 1986

After the first few minutes, there was little silence during the service. The words spoken were heartfelt words that told of a 38-year-old man who had touched the lives of children and their parents, quadriplegics and other patients, alcoholics, men in trouble, single parents, hospital personnel, friends, family and so on. We were amazed and touched, for although we saw Chris as a man of good will, we had not realized how wide a swath of caring he had cut.

Penny, Chris's girlfriend, read the chorus of a song Chris had written:

I'm a friend when
You need someone to talk to,
I'm a lover when
You need someone to squeeze you,
I'm a stranger when
You need to find what's true,
Babe, I wanna be good to you.

from *Friend, Lover and Stranger*
a song by Chris Griffith

And then she said, "The song really says who Chris was, not just to me, but to everyone who knew him. He wanted to be there for everyone, sometimes to the exclusion of not being there for himself. . . . He was the kindest person I have ever known. . . ."

After the service there was food for everyone. An Irish folk music group, some of Chris's favorite musicians, played and sang. People came to us and spoke of their sorrow. It was as healing a time as it could possibly be. Thanks to the combined efforts of Chris's friends and Columbia Friends Meeting, many people grieving for Chris were in this place at the same time to weep and console one another.

Then it was time to leave. Wanda and Roy, my sister and her husband, Pam, my niece, and her young son, Woody, came back from Columbia to be with us the following day for the visitation at the meetinghouse.

We arrived home, exhausted. We felt very cared for by our own family, by our friends and by Chris's friends. It was as if each of them, in addition to their own pain, wished to take some of the incredible burden upon themselves. In writing about that day, I ended with "... and we bless them for it, every one."

Chris with People

In Chris's later years, he not only put more energy into his friendships in Columbia, he also spent more time with family and friends in Kansas City, Iowa, South Carolina, and elsewhere.

Holidays with the Folks. He usually spent holidays at home. We, his parents, trying to be unselfish, encouraged him to spend time with friends if that seemed a good thing for him to do. In this effort, we must have failed, for most Thanksgivings and Christmases Chris arrived on our street in his battered orange Datsun pick-up (until the Toyota entered his life).

We would listen for the sound of the truck and the slam of the door. Chris would lope up the walk, his long legs propelling him toward the house, a smile planted on his face even before he reached the door, bearing a hodgepodge assortment of possessions — a bulging, battered suitcase (sometimes two), a guitar (in the last year or two he left an extra guitar at our home especially for his visits), a laundry bag (deposited in the basement later to do in spare moments), and whatever else he thought appropriate for that particular holiday. And then with real enthusiasm in his voice, he would proclaim his arrival with a "Hi, Mom. Hi, Dad," and dropping his collection in the middle of the floor, sweep us into his arms. It was a joyful St. Bernard-puppy-type of greeting.

We are grateful for this memory, saddened that it is relegated to a place of what has been. Even yet, when the holidays roll around, there is the lingering ache of missing Chris. In that respect, as in many others in our lives, things will never be the same.

Christmas. At Christmas, Chris, like some of the rest of us, never quite made peace with gift-giving. Sometimes he approached Christmas shopping with dread, sometimes he avoided it altogether, and then there were the times we all received carefully selected gifts (never expensive — Chris had that thrifty streak) and we could feel his eyes upon us, hopeful that we would find his offering as appropriate as he did.

A Special Thanksgiving. "Dad, I've always wanted to hear more about when you were in prison. What was it like? What happened to you there?" Chris looked at John with a determined look and a twinkle in his eye. We had just finished breakfast on a morning during a Thanksgiving holiday in the mid-seventies. The table had been cleared and we were sitting around nursing a second cup of coffee. Those present were Chris, his current girlfriend, another of our sons (I can't remember which), John and me.

John, from South Carolina, had, at the age of nineteen, decided he could not participate in war and had refused to register for the draft. Sentenced in November of 1942, he had spent two years in prison in federal penitentiaries in Virginia and Kentucky.

We hadn't had a philosophy in earlier years about how to approach this episode in their father's life with our sons; I have a feeling we didn't talk about it much until their teen years. By that time, they recognized, I'm sure, that such a stand on the draft was uncommon and not accepted in most circles. We had lived during most of their growing-up years in that small, conventional farming community in Iowa. And though we hadn't made a secret of John's having been in prison, it wasn't something that came up in ordinary conversation, either.

When Chris first broached the subject of prison that morning, John held back. With the first words out of Chris's mouth, I thought, "Chris, you won't get anywhere with that." In the past I had found John close-mouthed on the subject.

"Oh, you don't want to hear about that," John said. But Chris persisted, and under his dogged and surprisingly skillful leading, I suspect John that morning talked about things he had never talked about before. I know I learned a lot. From his father, Chris extracted the thrilling story of a youth who decided to take seriously the commandment "Thou shalt not kill" by defying a law of the society in which he lived, a law he felt would lead to death for other human beings. The story of life in prison for a conscientious objector in the forties was not a pleasant one.

I'll never forget the look of awe in Chris's eyes as the story developed. "Oh, Dad, now that's something. And what happened next?" And he looked around the table to see if the rest of us were as fascinated as he was with what he was hearing. Satisfied, he pushed on, "And then what did you do?" "And what was it like in the hole?" "And how did you feel toward the guards?" And on and on.

Several hours later we got up from the table, exhausted, aware that we had traveled together to another time and that we had had a glimpse inside another John — the youth who dared to be different because of a principle, a stubborn young man who, because of a conscience that would not let him do otherwise, had endured two years of being locked up with all kinds of lawbreakers.

And it was all because of Chris's determination to hear the story that we had the chance to look back at that part of John's life.

I don't know whether it was a result of this conversation, or because of Chris's interest in men's issues, or something else, or all of the above — for whatever reason, Chris wrote a song in the early eighties called *Two Brothers* about two young men and war. It is a non-judgmental look at brothers and their decisions about war. The two brothers in the song are John and his older brother, Bob, who followed "different drummers" during World War II. Here are some of the verses of the song:

There were two brothers during World War II,
One went to prison and the other went to war,
Johnny went to prison saying, "I won't fight,"
Bobby went to war saying,"This war will end all wars."*

Johnny went down to the prison deep,
Johnny ate bread and water in the dark,
Johnny didn't follow the rules,
Did Johnny ever cry behind prison walls?

Bobby charged on the beachhead,
Bobby dove to the sand,
Bobby watched his friends die,
Did Bobby ever cry on the beachhead?

Johnny, you're now sixty years old,
Do you still feel those prison walls?
Do you feel all alone?
Do you wish for clarity?

Bobby, you're now sixty-two years old,
Do you still dive to the floor?
Do you feel all alone?
Do you wish for clarity?

Johnny and Bobby, talk together,
Johnny and Bobby, hug one another,
Johnny and Bobby, show your love,*
Why do they always pick on the young?
Why dc they always pick on the young?

---

*While "war to end all wars" is a phrase from World War I, Chris uses poetic license here in attributing the words to Bobby. Also, Chris would be the first to affirm that love between Bobby and Johnny did not falter at the time of World War II or at any other time.

Other Visits with the Folks. Chris came to visit us other times than holidays. Sometimes he talked about his problems: How could he be more decisive? Was he in the right profession? Should he remarry? How could he, one individual, make the world a better place? And of course, sometimes he played his music for us.

Near the end of his life, he often talked about his feelings on men's issues, violence, homosexuality, peace, women's issues. For him, these forays into philosophy were not idle engagements in words, they were serious attempts to make sense out of life — his life and the lives of others. For he was a sensitive young man living in a world full of insensitivity from one person to another. The extent of this insensitivity was part of his own death experience.

I remember the time he visited us when I was in a cast from ankle to hip for six weeks, having broken my kneecap. One weekend soon after the accident, he made the trip from Columbia to help me learn how to use crutches and just to cheer me up. He was good at both those things.

While John went to Quaker meeting that Sunday, Chris stayed home with me. After meeting and before John came home, two friends from Friends Meeting came to visit. We talked for a while and then Chris asked them if they would like to sample the potato soup he was making for lunch. When they said yes, he hustled out to the kitchen, dished up steaming bowls of soup for us all, and we sat there in the living room chatting and eating the soup. I was pleased with his easy hospitality with my friends. It still brings a burst of pride to my heart and tears to my eyes to recall the potato soup incident. I wonder if I ever properly conveyed my pleasure to him.

It's tempting when there's a person with expertise in the family to get what you can from him or her. We tried not to pester Chris, the physical therapist, with our pains, though sometimes we did ask for his counsel. We said, "Uh, Chris, I have this pain in my back. Got any suggestions? It's right here, no, lower, no, to the left." "And my neck. I have this little crick in my neck." Before he knew it, he was involved with our pain. And I believe he was pleased to help. He gave us pointers about back care that we still use.

Then there was the great experiment. "Now it says here . . ." Chris read from his manual. "Hold still," he admonished John, as he moved his hands over various pressure points of John's body. Chris had just studied acupuncture in an internship here in Kansas City. He was very interested in it, and like most devotees of something new, he was anxious to apply his knowledge. He thought it just might help John's failing hearing, and John was willing to be a guinea pig. Equipped with elementary knowledge and equipment, Chris, with great patience and hope, reading as he went along, performed some simple acupuncture.

Well, we entertained notions of a miracle because for a very short time (overnight), John's hearing improved some. But it didn't last. Chris was disappointed at not being able to help his dad.

Visits with His Auntie. My sister, Wanda, and brother-in-law, Roy, treasure visits they had from Chris. They live on the farm where my sister and I grew up near Earlham, Iowa, and Chris sometimes stopped there on the way to or from somewhere. My sister recalls the time he brought a big basket he had purchased for her in an antique store ("it is now *gold* to me"). He was concerned that the handle was not quite perfect.

She also writes of the "I really want a mule" incident. ". . . One time when Chris visited us he was living in a backwoods place near Columbia and he had decided he wanted a mule. Knowing Roy had horses he came for counsel. Now it's difficult for a man with Arabian horses to even think 'mule.' Roy took him to a fancy Arabian horse farm to see some really fine horses. As the owners were parading their best stock, Chris said in a loud voice, 'These are really fine horses, but I really want a mule.' There was stunned silence. Later Chris and Roy had such fun telling about it. I don't believe Chris ever owned a mule except on the Christmas and birthday cards we sent him from then on."

Chris and the Osborns. The Osborns, cousins of mine in a Quaker entanglement of relationships too complicated to explain here, lived a few miles from us when we lived in Napier. Nancy Osborn remembers visits Chris made to Ames in the seventies: "Like a very tall pixie, Chris seemingly had the propensity to show up when he was most needed. In the year after Daddy (Al Osborn) died (1978–1979) he stopped by more than once to visit Mom on his trips back up to Iowa; those visits were so special to her. Then, just as we were in the final throes of getting her things packed up to move her to her new house at Earlham, Chris showed up 'out of the blue' with his pick-up truck and said, 'Hi, what can I do?' Just like a guardian angel; how did he know just exactly when we needed him most?"

He Goes to Kentucky. Chris also visited with Ron and Rachel Knight in Kentucky. Ron is my nephew whose birthday is twenty days before Chris's. Rachel writes about the time Chris arrived at their log house and they weren't home. It was cold in the house, and thinking he would get a fire started in the wood-burning stove, Chris kindled the fire with a pile of wooden roof shingles he found near the stove. Fortunately, Ron has a good sense of humor for the shingles were some he had cut by hand to put on their roof. Later that evening Rachel recalls that Ron and Chris stayed up late playing music and singing. She remembers going to sleep to Chris singing *Ten Years Ago* and "that has been one of my favorite songs ever since."

The Standings Gather for a Reunion. In June of 1985 the Standings, descendants of George and Deborah Standing who emigrated from England and settled on a farm near Earlham, Iowa in 1870, held a reunion at Bear Creek Meetinghouse, only a mile from where George and Deborah brought their family of boys over a hundred years before. George and Deborah were my father's grandparents. Much to our delight, Chris attended this reunion with us.

He had a wonderful time visiting, singing and learning about his forbears. For him, who he was and where he came from had become important. He volunteered to take care of his grandma, Lydia Thompson, a responsibility he assumed with great tenderness and good humor, much to their mutual enjoyment.

He took part in the Standing talent show, singing and playing his guitar. His original song, *Indigo Bunting Morning,* was a big hit with the 150 or so relatives who assembled there. The chorus goes like this:

> It's an indigo bunting morning,
> It's an indigo bunting day,
> My mama she taught me how to pray
> And my daddy how to work all day.
> Now I don't laugh all that much
> But when I do it's a bunch,
> I'm as happy as a meadowlark
> On this indigo bunting day.
> I'm as happy as a meadowlark,
> And a puppy dog's bark,
> On this indigo bunting day.
>
> from *Indigo Bunting Morning*
> a song by Chris Griffith

The last verse of the song, printed at the beginning of this chapter, especially touched us as we thought about it later.

And always that weekend at the reunion, Chris looked out for Grandma, frequently taking her back to the house to rest. There is no way to get into the meetinghouse without going up two sets of steps so Chris helped her up and down those steps, tactfully allowing her to hold onto the railing and do as much for herself as she could.

On Saturday of the reunion we each were asked to stand and tell something about ourselves. There is a tender photo of Chris standing over to the side of his Grandma as she is trying to speak. There he is, six foot four, arms across his chest, an adoring smile on his face. And there she is, barely five foot two, with puzzled expression, her wavy white hair a little askew. It is obvious he is there in case she falters, for by this time communication had become difficult for her because of repeated small strokes, and yet unbeknownst to us, Parkinson's disease. This photo is in a collage of Chris on our mantel. I like to remember that day when they stood together. Now both of them are gone.

A Letter from Chris. Another item from Rachel Knight was a quotation from a letter Chris wrote her when she and Ron were having some problems in 1985. The letter, dated September 19 says in part, "I would like to inform you that I am writing this letter with an 'enchanted' pen. It always says something profound. It was given to me by Granddad and Grandma Thompson. Perhaps you have one of these pens. Plastered on the side of the pen in red letters is 'A DAY OF WORRY IS MORE EXHAUSTING THAN A WEEK OF WORK.' Oh, never, never have truer words been spoken. I know!!! I have a Ph.D. in worrying . . .

"One thing I get down on myself about regards decisions — trying to make the perfect decision. But I am beginning to learn that there is no perfect decision. Every path leads to many roads. Each road has beautiful scenery and its own hard knocks. You've got to give yourself the right to make a decision and realize that you can live with that decision as long as you are truly sensitive about what you want."

A First and Last New Car. In 1985, Chris for months tossed around the idea of buying a new car to replace his old orange Datsun pick-up. Most of his close family and friends were consulted. He was attached to the Datsun and he didn't like spending money. However, it had developed a holey floor in the front and was not as trustworthy for trips (even to Kansas City) as he would have liked. On September 11, 1985, he wrote, "Well, I have been thinking about buying a new Toyota Tercel station wagon. I was wondering whether you could do me a favor and price out the wagon in K.C. . . ." Chris and his father were alike in their pursuit of bargains. He wrote also in that letter, ". . . Life has been going quite well for me . . . John is doing fine . . . He sure is fun to live with . . . I am still looking at property to buy but not as hard . . ." It wasn't long after that letter that he bought a brand-new (a first for him) silver Toyota Tercel station wagon (in Columbia!). He wrote out a check for the total cost of the car. Without this new conveyance, he wouldn't have made some of the trips he took in the last year of his life. He thoroughly enjoyed his new car, quickly forgetting how much it cost.

He Visits South Carolina Relatives and Friends. In June of 1986, the summer before his death, Chris and girlfriend Penny took a trip to South Carolina where they visited Grandmommie Griffith in Greenville, S.C. and Bob and Ann and members of their family who lived in or near Georgetown. Georgetown is located just up the coast from Charleston and is near Pawley's Island where Bob and Ann's beach house is located. Chris and Penny romped in the ocean as Chris had so often done as a child and visited places we had seen on our many trips to South Carolina. They went to Charleston, and he visited the hospital where for a year he had trained. He had a grand time renewing all these acquaintances and checking out his memories.

His Uncle Bob wrote later: "I am thankful that we had a visit with Chris and that he had visited other relatives and friends in the same time period. I had known that Chris was an outstanding young man. The outpouring of tributes to Chris at the memorial service in Columbia by many of his friends made me know that he was truly exceptional in his love and service to mankind."

He Visits Grandma Thompson and Goes to a Class Reunion. In July, Chris visited my mother and stepdad near Paullina, Iowa and also went to his twentieth high school class reunion near Boone, Iowa. First he drove to Mom's in northwest Iowa, arriving there in the middle of the night and sleeping in his car until morning so that he wouldn't disturb my mom and stepdad. He spent that day with them and then drove to Boone, some 170 miles southeast that evening for his reunion.

Joyce Osborn, his classmate and cousin writes, "The last time I saw Chris was at our twentieth high school reunion — I was *so* relieved to walk in and see him there. He really seemed to enjoy himself and visited freely with everyone. . . ."

Later that evening Joyce and Chris both went to spend the night with Nancy (Joyce's sister) in Ames. Nancy writes, "Chris spent that night on my living room sofa sleeper, and the next morning we three chatted easily over a breakfast of muffins and eggs with salsa, a selection he said was 'one of my all-time favorites . . .' "

Serendipity or What? We didn't see Chris after that trip to Iowa so didn't get to discuss that adventure with him in person. In telephone conversations with him, it was apparent he enjoyed being at the reunion. He had a new concern about Grandma;

he was sure, even though it hadn't been diagnosed by her doctors, that she had Parkinson's in addition to her strokes. Later, shortly before her death, this was confirmed by a doctor.

It is interesting to note that Chris had all these contacts with family and friends, some of whom he hadn't seen for years, in the last two years of his life. Call it serendipity, fate, or whatever you will. We heard from many of these people after his death; they spoke of their joy at seeing him, their happy memories of his visit; and with us, they mourned his death.

Another memory of the last summer in Chris's life comes from Tim. "The last time I saw Chris was at a Royals baseball game. I can remember feeling grouchy during the game and on the ride home. Mom and Dad were irritating me, Chris was irritating me, and Jason was irritating me. I was poor company. I still felt grouchy the next day and didn't try very hard to have personal contact with Chris before he went back to Columbia. Several days later, I really felt bad about how I had acted during his visit. I called him in Columbia and shot the bull for a while. When it was time to say good-bye I said, 'Chris, I love you.' He answered that he loved me, too. That was the last conversation we had."

Chapter Nine

ASHES

No, children should bury parents,
This order is wrong.

You knew of our plans,
Where our ashes should lie.

We do not know of yours, my son.

For it is too soon,
Your season has not come,
It is not time for you to die.

They say you are gone;
We are alive,
Perplexed and unbelieving.

What is this cruel hoax,
This cosmic error,
That thrusts your ashes into our hands?
— Reva Griffith, September 1986

On Sunday, the day after the memorial service in Columbia, most of those at our house attended Penn Valley Meeting of Friends, the religious community for John and me for twenty years. That day, the meeting for worship was not a typical Friends meeting, for the tragedy in our lives was upon the hearts of everyone present. It became a meeting of ministry to us as we sought to begin to make sense of the tragedy of Chris's death. We were surrounded by love.

At that meeting John said, "When one experiences the type of tragedy that our family has lived through the past few days it is inevitable, I suppose, that the mind will grope in confusion to understand the event. One wonders how a compassionate God can apparently be so indifferent to what happens to people . . .

"Our family has hurt deeply in this experience. But with the hurt there has emerged for me a perception in which I see more clearly than ever the need to be open to the power of love which is in each of us — and the need to introduce that love into all of our relationships. This is what Chris's life was about. And in the deepest silence of my spirit, I know that a murderer's bullet can in no way diminish the spiritual essence of Chris or the power of love which found expression in his life."

There was a visitation for our family that afternoon at the meetinghouse. We were surprised by the number of people who came to be with us — friends and relatives from Iowa; Quakers from Kansas, Iowa and Nebraska; former co-workers of us both; current co-workers of Tim; community people we knew. Penn Valley Friends served refreshments and took care of what little formality was needed. It was a moving and comforting event for us all. Had we known there would be so many people, we might have arranged for another memorial service in Kansas City in a larger building. However, for John and me, since the meetinghouse has been the center of our lives here in Kansas City, it seemed the appropriate place to be.

Then the exodus of family was upon us. Mary, John's niece, and her husband, Jeff, had begun the long trek back to Boulder that morning, and my sister and her family left that evening. The circle that had bound us together as we grieved, got meals and took care of one another through those heartbreaking days was broken.

On Tuesday, family members remaining in Kansas City — Tim, Jon, Ben, Ron and Bob and Ann — went with us to Columbia to face the problem of what to do with the rest of Christopher's things. Bill took the never-used water bed as agreed before, and in addition to the picnic table, Penny would get the truck at a later time after we'd hauled Chris's things home; Claire, who was going to move into the house, would get the refrigerator; others were given things they especially wanted. Ben and Ron packed some of Chris's possessions they wanted in their station wagon since they were leaving for Kentucky that day from Columbia.

Chris's remaining personal belongings — some small items of furniture, the bike he prized so highly, odds and ends of all kinds that meant something special to us or to him — these things we packed into his orange Datsun truck to take to Kansas City. We left large furniture, some books and kitchenware for Claire to sell in a garage sale to benefit BRAVO. John and I went to the bank, visited Chris's colleagues at work and did other errands while the rest packed the boxes. Ann had put together a delicious lunch from the food friends had brought to our house; this we ate once more for the last time on the picnic table.

Then we left the house, the place where Chris had resided peacefully, though not especially neatly, with the simple, somewhat broken-down, furnishings that he required to carry on the business of living. His treasures would have sold cheaply for they were not the treasures of the world. They were treasures of the heart — pictures painted by his grandfather; tapes of music by composers, some well-known, others obscure; three guitars of varied value; simple art pieces from places he had been; quilts made by his grandmother; an ancient stereo; a black-and-white TV (seldom used); camping gear. "Even yet," I wrote later, "it amazes and angers me to think that one man's death can matter so much to his family and friends and yet we can in one short day move the possessions he held dear from his home to new locations."

We said a tearful good-bye to Ben and Ron after lunch as they took off for Kentucky. By late afternoon, our sad caravan — a heavily laden orange Datsun truck and Christopher's much-loved silver Toyota wagon — began to wend its way back to Kansas City.

The next day we reluctantly put Jon on a plane for Austin. Our out-of-town residence family had dwindled to Bob and Ann. They stayed for another week, giving comfort, helping us with whatever we thought needed to be done, giving us time alone with someone who cared near at hand. On their trips out of the house, they saw Kansas City sights and bought groceries, especially white grapes which we all found bolstered our spirits. They urged us to go with them to hear former President Carter speak at a Habitat for Humanity rally at Barney Allis Plaza downtown. We went, making a first step back into life outside our grief. The presence of Bob and Ann helped to cushion our entry into a world without Chris.

Then they left. They seemed to have instinctive knowledge of the moment when we needed to get on with our grief alone. Their ministry to us, as we began the long process of going on, was a priceless never-to-be-forgotten gift.

Now the loneliness of grief was closing in.

Chapter Ten

CHRISTOPHER'S SONG

Christopher, this song's for you,
How I wish I could sing it to you
But you're lying still, cut down by the bullet
From a madman who didn't even know you,
And Christopher, this song's for you,
I heard a voice coming from you
Through a crippled child with cerebral palsy
Who didn't know my tears from her wheelchair,
She only laughed when I mentioned you.

Christopher, brother and friend,
You showed me how to be a new man,
He flexes his feelings instead of his biceps
And opens his heart instead of his wallet,
Manhood now stands there, a balance secure.
Christopher, I play your guitar,
I sing of love with your patience so true.
Forgive us our sadness, forgive us our anger,
And forgive our lost chances of loving you better,
But Christopher, we now live in you,
We will begin our whole lives anew.
They say that a best friend will lay down his life
So the other one can go on living,
I live in that joy, and really do miss you.

— a song by Ben Griffith, September, 1986

Our minds were so occupied with Chris's death in those first weeks that much of the time we didn't associate it with a crime. However, the media did. At first I planned not to read or listen to any of it. Then the need to know drove me to the newspapers. There were headlines and articles in morning and evening papers every day until, and even after, the arrest of the man accused of the murder.

POLICE SEEK CLUES IN QUADRUPLE MURDER
— *Columbia Daily Tribune*, September 10, 1986

FOUR FOUND SLAIN IN WILDLIFE AREA
— *Kansas City Times*, September 10, 1986

KILLINGS OF 4 CALLED 'HIT AND GO'
— *Kansas City Star*, September 10, 1986

INVESTIGATORS SIFT CLUES IN SEARCH FOR KILLER
— *Kansas City Star*, September 11, 1986

SEARCHING FOR AN EXPLANATION
— *Kansas City Times*, September 11, 1986

FEW CLUES IN MURDER OF 4
— *St. Louis Post-Dispatch*, September 11, 1986

CORONER OFFERS DETAILS OF RANGE KILLINGS
— *Columbia Daily Tribune*, September 12, 1986

FOUR SHOT AT CLOSE RANGE, AUTOPSIES FIND
— *Kansas City Times*, September 12, 1986

'BULLETS BY THE HUNDREDS' HINDER CASE
— *St. Louis Post-Dispatch*, September 12, 1986

And so on.

From Chris's friends, co-workers and through the papers we learned that on that black day Chris, who was staffing a new program on back care at Rusk Rehabilitation Center, had gone with James Watson, safety specialist with the Missouri Conservation Department, to Blind Pony Fish Hatchery near Sweet Springs, Missouri in the morning. Through Rusk, Chris had a contract as a consultant to the Conservation Department to study ways to ease back strain for the employees at the fish hatchery. He arrived at his office at Rusk in time to see one patient, a child, before he left.

He and James Watson then drove to Sweet Springs in a Conservation Department car, where they observed the work at the hatchery and talked with the workers, visited with the staff, had lunch, and then left in the early afternoon to return to Columbia. On the way back, Watson, in his capacity as safety specialist, apparently decided to check on the shooting range while he was nearby so they left the Interstate at the Marshall exit, driving down a winding gravel road to the Marshall Junction Wildlife Area where the shooting range is located. Law enforcement officials theorized that they arrived sometime before 3:00 P.M. just as someone was putting the bodies of two men, brothers-in-law Donald Vanderlinden from Independence and John Burford from Sedalia, into Mr. Vanderlinden's car.

Officials believed Chris and Watson were shot because they "were at the wrong place at the right time." Wallets of all the men except for Chris were gone so they also judged the original motive was robbery. Vanderlinden and Burford, about to go on vacation, were reported to have been carrying a large amount of cash.

A special group of law enforcement officers from eleven counties and the highway patrol, forty-five in all, were called in to investigate the murders. The papers described the scene of the murders and the shooting range in vivid terms. The clues found at the scene were shell casings, blood, fingerprints, an unopened pack of Marlboro cigarettes. All four men were shot more than once at close range. Over 140 leads were checked out in the course of the investigation. Reward money from several different sources was offered.

The Columbia papers carried several articles about Chris. These articles comforted us as the horrible reality of his death unfolded in the news media.

> *Columbia Daily Tribune, September 11:* "... those who knew Griffith describe him with words like 'extraordinary,' 'outstanding,' even 'magical.' And they grieve that a man who gave so much of himself to others should give up his life for no good reason at all."
>
> *Columbia Daily Tribune, September 14, letter to the editor:* "... His gentle strength touched people all over Columbia, in a number of settings, over many years. His music, his smile, his sense for children's potentials, his constant willingness to listen and offer his support and friendship will all be missed.
>
> "But what our community will miss most is the loss of a quietly powerful force lobbying for nonviolence. The need for people like Chris is great. People who believe that violence is unacceptable in all settings: our schools, work places, Columbia streets and, especially, our homes ..."
>
> — Dr. Coleen Kirlahan, Medical Director of the Boone County Health Department
>
> *The Missourian, September 14:* "Seeing him with little kids, he was sort of a gentle giant — comparing his height to the kids."
>
> — Barbara Colin, mother of a child with Down's Syndrome treated by Chris
>
> *Columbia Daily Tribune, September 10, feature article entitled "Griffith Remembered as a Man of Peace":* "A devotee of folk and old-time music, Griffith played

> guitar and participated in area folk-dance groups. 'He was a gentle kind of fellow,' remembered a man who played music with Griffith. 'He believed everyone was good.'..."

While we looked at the news to see what was going on in the case, we felt a kind of detachment from it all. It seemed to be about someone else. The only really relevant thing to us was that Chris had been killed. It was almost as if Chris's death happened without a perpetrator. That it had happened was all that really engaged our attention.

On Monday evening, September 15, Donald Edward Reese, a forty-three-year-old Marshall truck driver, was arrested and charged with four counts of first-degree murder, three counts of first-degree robbery and four counts of armed criminal action. Several clues at the shooting range pointed to him. The murder weapon was a .30-caliber rifle and Reese could not produce his .30-caliber rifle because he "had just sold it to an unknown stranger." Reese's wife had left him two weeks before, taking their two sons with her; she had returned the morning of September 9 to pick up two doghouses and there had been a fight. It was also learned that Reese had financial problems.

On Tuesday evening after the arrest, acting on information given them by Reese, law officers searched for and found the murder weapon in a creek in southeast Saline County; the three missing wallets were found buried in the mud of the creek nearby. Reese had drawn the map that led law officers to the wallets. In a heavily overgrown area near a rock quarry where he had been employed, searchers were directed by Reese to a tin can containing hundred dollar bills; a total of $2,300 was recovered from two locations.

Reese dictated a five-page statement to authorities. He said he had been at the firing range the afternoon of September 9 target shooting. Two men pulled up and got out of the car with rifles. He talked with them for several minutes and then went back to his own car. While sitting on the hood of the car, he said, his finger on the trigger accidentally discharged the rifle, shooting one of the men. The other man started to come toward him, and he had to shoot him. He put their bodies and one of their rifles in their car and was going back for the other rifle when a car with two men (Watson and Chris) drove into the shooting range and parked near the other car. He thought Watson had seen the victims as he got out of the car, and started shooting at him. Chris got out of the car on the other side and ran toward the wooded area; Reese shot at him as he ran into the woods where he fell, mortally wounded.

Reese then got into his car and drove toward the creek some distance away where the wallets were found; he took the money from the wallets, and then buried them and threw the rifle into the creek. Such a simple, matter-of-fact story, yet what happened to the four victims brought excruciating heartbreak to four families and Reese's own family and changed all of our lives forever.

With the arrest and arraignment, the process of moving toward a trial of the accused was put into motion. The Missouri Rural Major Case Squad was disbanded after an eight-day investigation.

As I read back over the history of those few days, I wonder that we survived. Yet, as we have talked with others who have been similarly involved in tragedy, most people seem to find the strength to do what they have to do, to absorb horror and postpone pain. The pain comes, but mercifully, not all in one dose. I read in the papers how Chris died and it was brutal and I knew it; it wasn't until later that I allowed myself to see and feel the full horror of it.

IF ONLY . . .

If only I had been there
To hold your head in my lap,
To comfort you in your pain,

I cannot bear to think of you
Dying in that place you did not know
From the hand of a man you did not know,
A man who bore you no ill will,
Except that you were there.

No, I will redo the scene,
You escape into the woods,
He drives away,
Or the shots go awry,
Or he decides he's had enough
Of killing,
And spares you.

It is not so,
That's not the way it was.
For some unbearable reason,
He fired the gun.

Then I wish instead
I had been there
To hurl myself between you,
To take the shots he meant for you.

So that you had not fallen
Beside that bridge,
In those woods,
Unsuspecting,
Innocent.
Alone.

— Reva Griffith, December, 1986

During the weeks following the departure of our family (except for Tim and his family here in Kansas City), we busied ourselves with the leftovers of Christopher's life. We sorted his possessions, trying to think of family and friends who might like particular things; we wanted them in the hands of those who cared for him. I washed all his clothes and folded them or hung them up on hangers, even mending some of them. John went through his papers, made telephone calls to determine how to settle his estate. Our activity felt like an extension of our love for Chris; the busyness of dealing with his possessions and affairs was really the only kind of work we cared to do.

Each day we waited for the click of the mailbox; we opened the letters that poured in, grateful for friends and family who cared, passing the messages across the table to one another. They brought tears but the tears washed at the pain; others loved and grieved for Chris as well as we. The letters cradled us, soothing the rawness of our spirits.

> *9/12/86* ... I am comforted when I remember that spirit can't be killed, that Chris related to everyone, not in terms of their physical condition, not in terms of male or female, not in any ordinary earthly sense. Rather he chose to touch every other spirit, to recognize and uplift even the most discouraged of us, with his own grand, smiling, and hope-filled spirit.
>
> — Young woman whose child was a patient of Chris

> *9/24/86* ... I feel the love Christopher gave to all of us is multiplying and surrounding those of us who were a part of his life as we reach out and comfort each other.
>
> — A good friend of Chris's

> *9/30/86* ... Chris was sure a nice man. I will miss him. I just want to write and tell you I feel so bad and I'm thinking of you and your family.
>
> — Patient of Chris's six years earlier

10/13/86 ... Chris, I remember was so gentle and kind to everyone around him. ... I guess that's what upsets me about his death. It's so ironic the way it happened. We will miss him dearly.

— Mother of a child who was
a patient Columbia Public Schools

9/30/86 ... He was truly one of a kind ... please know that I am just one of many that have thought of

Columbia Daily Tribune
Sept. 10, 1986

Three months before his murder yesterday, Chris Griffith is shown in this *Tribune* file photo working with a physically impaired child at New Haven Secondary School. "He was outstanding," a school official recalls. "To work with children like that, you need to have not only skill but compassion."

nothing else except Chris since this horrible thing happened.

— Patient of Chris at Rusk

10/22/86 ... I recall many hot summer nights hanging out on the porch swing listening to Chris's sweet, clear voice as he strummed away on the guitar (his kittens at his feet).

— A friend

Perhaps one of the reasons we immersed ourselves in Chris so totally was because we were retired and home all day; or maybe it was just the way we were; or maybe most people react this way and we had never noticed. Some folks said, "How can you stand to not be occupied with work or something outside the house to take your minds off this thing?" How could we take our minds off something that tore at the center of our beings?

YOUR FATHER AND I

We are caught in a moment of time,
Your father and I;
The moment you died.

We sort through your things;
Caress your garments;
Try to feel you there.

We play the tape of your songs,
Hear your strong, full voice,
Marvel at the man you were,
Imagine you before us, guitar in hand.

Sometimes we think we see you,
A tall, faceless man in a crowd;
And our paces quicken.
Oh, vain and foolish hope.

You left us at that bridge
As bullets rained about you.
When the rifle fell silent,
Pain and emptiness entered our lives.
— Reva Griffith, September, 1986

We learned as we went along that people grieve at different paces and in different ways and times. Most of us have to work through it some way. There is pain to be endured somehow; it can be set aside for awhile, absorbed in small doses, or one can take it as it comes. I suppose most of us combine all of the above. I wrote in June, 1988: "Grief . . . is a process that goes on as inexorably as the days pass. It is not over at a whim. We do not choose it; it is there to be endured, lived with and integrated into our lives." This has been our experience.

The weekend of October 3–5 we attended the Missouri Valley Friends Conference at Camp Chihowa near Lawrence, Kansas. We might not have gone except that I was clerk (presiding person) for that year and had been in charge of arrangements for the program of the conference. It seemed appropriate to go on with this part of our lives. So we went, and I, with much help from everyone, did my job. Fortunately for us, Elizabeth and George Watson, well-loved Quakers from Baltimore, were the resource persons for the conference. One of their daughters had been killed in an auto accident some years ago and Elizabeth had written a book, *Guests of My Life*, about her grief. They talked with us, sheltered us and soothed the rawness of our hearts.

In mid-October I was called to northwest Iowa to help care for my mother. It was hard to leave both John, Chris's other parent and my strength, and the remainders of Chris's life. It also postponed grieving for me as I shifted to my mother's problems — congestive heart failure, Parkinson's disease, small strokes.

The good aspect of it was that I had a chance to grieve with her. She was unable to talk and the pain she felt at Chris's death was apparent though unexpressed. Most of the time I tried to be cheerful as I cared for her. However, at one point I decided to tell her about the memorial service, about how much Chris was loved and appreciated, how much I loved and missed him but that I was going to be all right. She listened, understanding in her eyes, and tears came, as grief poured out for Chris and for me. I truly believe that talk helped her; and I know it helped me. She dearly loved Chris, all her grandchildren for that matter, and we needed to cry together. I stayed a few days with her after she got home from the hospital and then returned to Kansas City.

It was good to get back to John. However, I discovered that we were not grieving together anymore; he had gone on with his grief while I had been on "hold." I was upset to lose the closeness. We have since read and learned that this kind of situation is troublesome and normal with parents who lose children. There is a high incidence of divorce among couples who lose children by death.

After an emotional outburst one evening, I sat down and wrote a note to John, telling him how I felt. I was glad to learn later that he had kept the note in his Chris file. Some of what I wrote follows: "When I came back from caring for Mom, I felt a need to pick up where we left off. You, on the other hand, stated you felt a need to 'get on with life.' You seldom needed me as a comforter; I needed a comforter. . . . I was still 'tearing up' about Chris while you seemed to have skipped from emotional to logical . . .

"Also, I have felt confused about this whole thing of grief. It has been only two months since Chris suffered a horrible murder; yet I feel in myself and in you, our sons, and others, a beginning of acceptance of this thing. At the same time, my whole being cries out against our accepting it. So at times I have this incredible mixture of anger, guilt and horror and I don't know what to do with it. I know we have to get over it and go on with living, but I feel so outraged that I often work against that in myself and you."

A few thoughtful conversations helped get us to a place where we understood one another better. I think both of us became more conscious of the unevenness of this path we were on and resolved to be kind to one another as we stumbled along. Each of us had good and bad days, and they didn't always coincide with one another.

And so the days went on in those early months after Chris's death. I would often discover tears streaming down my face as I drove down a street; sometimes when driving the car I would pass a turn I had planned to make. When I took my daily walk, I thought of Chris — in fact, I couldn't keep from thinking of him — and I let the tears flow, not caring what passersby might think. A friend remarked that upon the death of his son several years before, he had felt compelled to tell people he met about it. I found myself behaving that way at times — it was as if I craved universal sympathy for this unbearable loss.

Concentration and memory deserted us both during those days. We tried to convince ourselves we were normal although we sometimes thought we were losing our minds. We felt as if we had bumped into a brick wall of pain and the pain would never end. It was a physical pain, often manifesting itself as a hurting lump in the stomach. Indeed John and I and all of our sons lost weight in the early weeks after Chris's death.

Without understanding and sympathy from friends, relatives and mere acquaintances, our loss would have been even harder to bear. Love and caring came to us in many forms — flowers, books, cards, plants, letters, calls, food, invitations, smiles, hugs, and ways we had not imagined (we learned there are many ways to say "I care") — and they steadied us as we tried to pick up our lives in the middle of this tragic sorrow, and go on.

Chapter Eleven

TEARS

Even the heavens are crying,
See — buckets of water pour from the skies,
By day clouds heavy with rain cover the sun,
And by night tears fall from hidden moon eyes.

And our tears flow;
Quiet rivers ooze from burning lids;
We breathe great gulping sobs;
We weep, my son, for you.

Tomorrow green earth will shimmer in the sun
And the moon will dry its tears,
Our sobs will quiet with the wind,
But tears for you will never cease.

— Reva Griffith, October, 1986

Then the first year without Chris began. We started down a path parents hope never to travel — the path of grief for a child. As our four sons grew up, I can remember thinking that I couldn't bear the loss of any of them. I had tried not to think of it over the years. But now it had happened. Chris was dead.

For parents (especially mothers) reality of the baby begins as she/he jostles along in the womb, a bonding personified with that first astonished cry. During childhood years, there is non-stop action. Endless feedings; hundreds of diapers to change; tears to stem with healing kisses; interminable instructions to issue on all sorts of subjects in all kinds of ways. There are pranks and laughter, thousands of cookies, quiet story hours at the end of a day, bikes, and balls, and school plays, and all the crises and pleasures that children bring wherever they are. Through those years, we build relationships bit by bit, word by word.

Then adolescence strikes and the real test begins. Will they survive? Will we survive? We all usually do, although the clash of wills sometimes leaves us battered.

In the years that follow, we negotiate the parameters of co-existence, and finally, with a little bit of luck, a more peaceful time emerges with the real possibility of friendship. This had happened with Chris.

> . . . Chris talked at length about how he had been to visit his parents recently, and told them things about himself which he had never before divulged, and that he felt he was moving toward the kind of adult-to-adult relationship he wanted.
>
> — Francis Baumli

As I have said before, in the days following Chris's death, both John and I found concentration on anything not connected with Chris very difficult. For awhile, doing the things we had to do was enough. Then a friend suggested we might find an organization called The Compassionate Friends helpful. TCF is a self-help group formed to help parents deal with the death of children. We hesitated, thinking it was probably geared to young parents, not the near elderly. However, we did decide to go, attending our first meeting several weeks after Chris's death.

We were greeted by a friend of a friend who was a member of the group. "Oh, you poor person," she said, "I am so sorry." And she put her arms around me.

The meeting began with all of us sitting in a large circle; there were probably thirty people there. There was a quiet introduction by one of the people who had been in the group for a while. She welcomed us, said she was glad we had come though sorry for the cause of our being there, told us that our behavior while at TCF would not be scrutinized, we could expect sympathy and understanding, no one would tell us what we ought to do or feel. Then we went around the circle, each person telling his/her name, the name of the child, the age, and cause of death. Anyone who couldn't handle this assignment was asked to touch the next person. John was before me. I remember the shock I felt as he said, "My name is John Griffith. My son's name was Christopher. He was 38 years old. He was murdered September 9." The fact of Chris's death was revealed to everyone there; a pulse of sympathy ran through the group. I passed. I think I could not have said anything.

Then we met in smaller groups where those who had been there before (some for several years) talked about their experiences and encouraged those who were there for the first time to share their pain. Tears were expected; comments were sympathetic; understanding was everywhere. Parents of all ages from all walks of life talked about their children and shared grief experiences with other parents.

In the first year, we went to most of the monthly meetings of The Compassionate Friends. Telling about Chris's death to this circle of friends became easier as the months went by; in fact, as we became acquainted with others in the group and became familiar with their stories, bonds were established that will never be forgotten.

In those early days, I wrote grief poetry; it helped for me to put the pain into words, to say exactly how it felt to me.

WHERE WERE YOU?

Where were you anyway —
Where were you when the bullet pierced his back?

Were you gazing into starry space?
Or lost in some great cosmic plan?

Or did you in that fateful second
Turn your head,
Avert your eye,
And let the slayer slay him?

Or are there accidents
Of time and space,
Celestial miscalculations?
Do you too, cry?

Or was this in your blueprint
All along?
Had it been writ before I bore him?

If so, why?
Why create a man like this
And then in moments,
Tear him down
Like a castle in the sand?

— Reva Griffith, September, 1986

We continued to do what was necessary to wrap up the material remains of Chris's life. Then one day most of the sorting of papers and possessions was done. The estate decisions had been made and a lawyer consulted. Ever so slowly we edged back into our former activities. At first, it required concentration to think of anything but Chris. Gradually it became easier to mix thoughts of him with tasks at hand. Chris was not forgotten — not at all — rather he had moved from center stage in our minds and was standing over to the side.

Fall became winter.

WINTER

Winter is coming,
The hills are stark,
Barren,
The trees
Loom naked against the sky.

And you are gone.

My heart is cold,
Cold as the wind that shivers across the prairie,
As the river that chatters
Under the ice.

For . . .
You are dead, my son,
And my heart may never be warm.

— Reva Griffith, November, 1986

Winter became spring, a different spring, a spring without Chris.

DOGWOOD DAYS

It is spring,
I know it is spring,
Pink and white flashes of dogwood
Jump out from behind the houses,
Yet, as I walk along the sidewalk
I am lost in a dream.

Dancing tulip faces, red and yellow,
Smile at me,
The sun's rays wrap 'round me
As cool velvet breezes touch my face,
I walk beside the trees,
Touching new green on the branches.

Warblers, robins, cardinals,
Blend in a crazy chorus,
But their songs are muted.

It is not the same this year.

I see the dogwood
Through a mist of sadness
For you, my son.

For, in the yard of your friend,
A dogwood blooms
In your memory.

— Reva Griffith, May, 1987

In the midst of our activity, we often stopped to muse, with profound regret and uncomprehending puzzlement, on the horrid event that had taken Chris's life. For him there was much left undone. He often talked of the possibility of getting married again, expressing a wistful hope that it would last this time; he spoke of perhaps having a child; he had plans for more school, maybe in counseling, to enhance his work in physical therapy and give him an even more satisfying career; he talked of travel to new places. In many ways, he had reached a comfortable place in his life; he had worked through much of the "stuff" from earlier years that gets in the way; he had good friends in Columbia and other places for whom he had great affection and whom he trusted with helping him to live more fully.

But he was unfinished; and we were unfinished with him — our son/friend.

Both of us dreamed of him and felt him close to us at times.

THE DREAM

Last night I dreamed of you,
I was in a room
Of shadowy persons
When suddenly,
There you were.
In the darkness of the place
There came a burnished glow
From the auburn of your hair,
Your smile was in the room,
You stood above the others,
There was a feel of gentleness
And quiet.

I knew you at once.

I called your name
And you opened your arms,
And, as I fell into them
They folded about me
Like angel wings,
I was happy.

And then, your arms grew limp,
I cried, "Please stay,
Stay to see your father."

But you faded and disappeared
Like a candle whose wick runs out,
Leaving nothing
But the brush of your gentleness
On my cheek.

— Reva Griffith, May, 1987

John has recorded several dreams he had in the year after Chris's death. Here are two of them.

October 16, 1986: I was in a room and Chris came in with a big smile and a cheerful "Hi, Daddy-o." I was very much aware that Chris was supposed to be dead and said, "Chris, what's this about? I don't understand what's going on." Chris could see that I was in great pain and said, "I'm sorry I haven't written, Dad, but I have been O.K." I had the feeling Chris wasn't dealing directly with the problem of our meeting and I said, "Chris, don't do this. I just don't know how much more I can take." Without any further conversation Chris came over and embraced me and we both cried.

February 13, 1987: This morning about 5:00 A.M. I had a dream about Chris. Chris suddenly appeared in the same room where I was. He seemed like his old self, was cheerful and acted as if nothing out of the ordinary was happening. We talked a short while with our arms around each other's shoulders. At this writing I do not recall what that conversation was about, but it was a typical, cheerful conversation with Chris. I was impressed that his body seemed totally normal. I said to him, "Chris, I don't understand this meeting with you. You are supposed to be dead but your body feels just like when you were alive. How is that possible?" Chris said, "Well, it isn't easy to get a pass but here I am." I said, "Chris, you know we love you and miss you." Chris put both his arms around me and said, "I know," and we both cried. I had the sense Chris was crying more for our sadness than for his.

From the first hours after Chris's death, I could not reconcile his death as being a part of a plan of a caring God. My faith in spiritual things, always tentative, though earnestly striven for, went through shaky times.

FAITH — STRIPPED

My faith has crumbled
Around my feet.
I have picked up the twisted pieces,
Looked at them one by one,
And found them wanting.

Yes, I have examined each piece,
Checked it for soundness
And marked it "Rejected."

What I have claimed as belief
Does not fit any more.

Yes, my faith has been stripped
Like a broken down car,
The vehicle built through the years
Has fallen into a heap.

— Reva Griffith, June 1987

Meanwhile, Christopher's friends kept in touch with us, and in some very special ways demonstrated their love for Chris.

In late 1986, Andrew Sieff, a friend of Chris's, published a tape of piano music entitled *My Wish for You*, written and played by Andrew. Inside the case where credits are given, he writes, "This music is dedicated to the memory and energy of Christopher Griffith, a gentle man who loved people and justice." We often listen to this soothing music as we travel in our car, remembering Chris and his friend, Andrew.

On March 1, 1987, a New Games Fest was held in Columbia. Partially inspired by memory of Chris, the flyer advertising the event read in part, "Michelle Emery was recently thinking of the violence in the world, particularly after the recent murder of our dear friend, Christopher

Griffith. We have been looking for more ways to heal after that experience ... so Michelle is getting a group of us together to play some games ..." Chris would have enjoyed the event and would have felt honored to have peaceful games played in his memory. For some now forgotten reason, we were unable to attend.

We attended a dedication ceremony April 1 for a painting and plaque donated to Rusk Rehabilitation Center in Chris's memory by some of his friends. In *Staff Life*, staff newsletter of the University of Missouri–Columbia Hospital and Clinics, Steve Johnson, one of the donors, was quoted as saying, "Essentially, we felt Chris was an unusually loving person and made an outstanding contribution to the community and to his personal friends. We wanted to do something to commemorate his life."

Diane Huneke, a Columbia artist who knew Chris, donated a watercolor painting of a torso in Christopher-like colors. Across it is a row of superimposed people holding hands; below them, are the words "My son, in you I am well pleased." It is a beautiful and fitting remembrance.

Several of Chris's friends put together the plaque. On it is a picture of Chris flashing his well-loved grin. Above his name are words from Gibran, "And when the earth shall claim your limbs, then shall you truly dance." Below the dates of his life, a caption reads, "Seeker of truth, Gentle spirit, Caring friend." We have since stopped in Columbia to see the painting and the plaque. We are still profoundly moved by this exhibit.

Early in 1987 we were contacted by Carmen Abbott, who was Chris's boss at Rusk Rehabilitation Center in Columbia. She wanted to know our reactions to a plan for a Christopher Griffith Memorial Run/Walk/Bike Event in the spring. It would benefit the Children's Miracle Network Telethon. There would be T-shirts and balloons and prizes. We were enthusiastic. What a wonderful way to remember Chris! Would we attend and take part? Yes, we would.

The day of the event, May 3, dawned wet and chilly. At the time the race was to start, a heavy shower began. However, it didn't last long and the race, though postponed half an hour, took place anyway. Cloudy and cool, the day proved a good one for a race after all. Fifty to sixty people (more had planned to participate but didn't come because of the rain) either ran or walked or biked the prescribed twelve-mile course. John finished the walk; I gave up after six miles.

After everyone was back (there was one accident; Chris's friend, Forrest, had a bike mishap and broke his hip), there was lunch and a presentation ceremony for the winners. John and I were treated like royalty; it did indeed help the mending to see so many people sporting Christopher Griffith Memorial T-shirts and having a good time in activities of which Chris would highly approve.

Grieving and healing, remembering and forgetting, holding to Chris and letting go of him — a delicate balance. All that year, we tried to respond to what seemed right for us as we moved along. We sometimes sensed in others a well-meaning wish for our return to how we were before. They wanted us well again. We gradually came to believe that our wellness would be different from the years before Chris's death. We sensed that as we emerged on the other side of the pain we would not be the same. However, we knew we had to move on; it was important for us and for those who cared for us.

THE PATH

At first
Friends, even strangers,
Came to us
To comfort us in our sorrow.

They walked near us
Touching us often,
Holding us in their hearts,
As we moved along
The early path of grief.

They remembered him with us,
Recognized our love for him,
Decried our great loss,
Gave us strength
To carry on.

Then, one by one,
Their voices faded,
And like parents of a child
Learning to walk,
They drew back.

As they should,
For we had to walk alone . . .
Sometime.

We do . . .

And there are moments
When the pain lessens,
Giving promise of one day
Dissolving into sweetness.

But often our hearts are sore
As we tread a ragged path
Littered with memories of him,
Scattered with his dreams,
And tangled with thoughts of
"Why?" and "what might have been."

— Reva Griffith, March, 1987

Through the months after Chris's death, my mother's health got worse. My sister and I and our husbands debated what to do. She was eighty-six in January of 1987; she lived in her own home with her second husband of ten years; he, though nearly ninety at the time, was well and kept a good house. A homemaker aide came in daily to bathe Mom and help our stepfather, Isaac, with her care. Still, more care was needed, care that required lifting her. We finally decided to put her in a nursing home near my sister in central Iowa. It was in the community where Mom had begun her married life with our father and much closer to Kansas City. She was there for ten days. On May 19, she died. This additional grief set me back for a while. Much of the time I didn't know for whom I was grieving. After an intense month or two, it eased.

In the spring after Chris's death, we had a call from the University of Missouri Medical School. Chris's ashes were at a funeral home in Columbia; we could pick them up. So we made another journey to Columbia one cloudy day, seeing it as one more part of caring for Chris. My nephew, Ron, a potter, had fashioned an urn of clay in which we stored the ashes.

We seriously considered a request made by Chris's Columbia friends that his ashes be put into Gans Creek, the place where he had spent many happy hours, and although the idea appealed to us, we decided we wanted to bury his ashes in a place we could visit.

We had a headstone made with his name, and ours, on it and placed it in the Quaker cemetery where my father and mother are buried, adjacent to the meetinghouse at Mapleside near Paullina in northwest Iowa. We had the burial when the weather was warm and when our three remaining sons could be present. The date agreed upon was June 20, 1987. I read the following poem at the burial.

ESSENCE

Here we are, my son,
We have come to this spot of not-so-long-ago prairie,

Where winter winds whip tiny snow crystals into graceful
white mounds,
And summer breezes make shimmering seas of emerald green
cornfields.

We bring your ashes, my son, to bury here
Near your forbears,
Your sweet grandma here only a month,
And your parents yet to join you.
It is time for us to do this.

Your ashes are light to carry
Though the burden of the heart is heavy.
We come with reluctant steps,

Unwilling to part with these particles,
Yet aware they have been only the carrier
Of the essence of you.

The essence of you we cannot describe,
For it is lost in words,
We feel it — a piece of each of us — forever.

We gather at this place,
Grieving, yet grateful
For your life and your love.

For the essence of you, my son.

— Reva Griffith, June, 1987

THE BURIAL

So we buried your ashes.

We sat in a circle
Around the marker of your grave,
The sun seeped through a muggy Iowa sky;

A light wind tickled the grass;
And we were silent.

Until one of us spoke
And then another
And another.
Each from our hearts,
Remembering
Your life
Your love
Your pleasure,
Expressing
Closeness to your spirit,
Faith in our memory of you,
Lingering pain at your death.

Then words ceased
And bit by bit,
Your father, brothers and I
Dropped your ashes into the earth,
Covered them with care,
Knowing, as we did, that they were only
The holders of your soul.

We listened to you sing your songs,
Now our songs,
And though the sound of your voice
Brought piercing pain,
The knowledge that you walked this earth
And sang of it
Comforted us.

Then we stood and formed a circle
Celebrating the moment
As we closed the earth on your ashes.

You are not gone, my son,

Your soul was not in the ashes,
It lingers in our hearts
As we go about our lives,
Missing you
Loving you
Yet,
And forever.

— Reva Griffith, July, 1987

Another piece of caring for Chris had been completed. Jon (Austin, TX) and Ben (Frankfort, KY) came to the burial; Tim had last minute work obligations that prevented his making the trip. Ben's wife, Patricia, and their little daughters, Treva and Carrie, were there as was Rosemary, Tim's now former wife. Present too were the close relatives who lived in the Mapleside Quaker community. It was a private, sad, and meaningful occasion.

Then there was Christopher's birthday July 25. John and I pondered how to spend the day. As a child, Chris got excited over birthdays and Christmas. What could we do to maintain a spirit of celebration on his thirty-ninth birthday?

I remembered his thirty-eighth birthday. I had called him a week or so before the day and asked, "Just what would you like for your birthday?" He thought for a few moments and then said, "Come see me one of these weekends." "Okay, we'll do it," I answered with every good intention in the world. "We'll probably send you a little something anyway." I mailed him a tape I thought he would like. And we really meant to visit him. We hadn't done it yet. Six weeks later he was dead.

To observe his thirty-ninth birthday, John and I decided to have dinner at Chris's favorite Kansas City Chinese restaurant. Then we rented the video of the movie *A Trip to Bountiful.* Chris, John and I had gone to that movie one of the last times he was home. We all loved it; John and I remembered how the three of us came out of the theater arm-in-arm, chatting about how Geraldine Page should win an Oscar for her role in that movie (which she did). It was a happy memory. We got through the day.

JULY 25, 1987

The day is here,
Your thirty-ninth birthday, my son,
Now nine months since your death.

I remember . . .
Hours of your childhood,
Days of your youth.
Moments of your life
Stand out
Like stars in a wintry sky,
Like diamonds on black velvet.
Your pain, my pain,
Your joy, my joy.

And I remember . . .
The day of your death,
The lights of the world turned off
For awhile.

I see them dimly now,
Only as the pain of your death
Dissolves into ongoing love for you.

Know, my son, your birth day
And all the days until your death
Were days when the earth
Turned in greater harmony
Because you were here.

— Reva Griffith, July, 1987

One of the questions people ask us is, "How do you feel towards the man who killed Chris?" I still don't know how to answer this question. My usual answer has been that we were so devastated by Chris's death that feelings toward this person were indistinct.

Several years ago Chris's youngest brother, Ben, shared with us poems he had written near the end of the first year. In these poems Ben deals directly with his anger. I am grateful that (1) he has expressed his anger; and (2) it awakens some of the denial in my own heart. His spewing out of the pain and anger that haunted us all may indeed have been the better approach. Here are these poems:

ANGER 1

One year to remember
how well you lived
and how painful your death.
Touching your picture
I realize that never again
you will pose that silly grin.

The cowboy that killed you
drove a truck, the paper says
he sits in prison drawing pictures of Jesus . . .
he doesn't remember (I suppose)
how the crowds at Golgotha
pierced your sides and head with bullets,
how the first bullet didn't bite you hard enough,
how fleeing from this mad world
(and three others lying dead)
with no chance but your martyrdom,
they hunted you down with no mercy
but save that of God's . . .
Dear Mr. Cowboy:
Jesus saves, but *you* must pay!

ANGER 2

I,
— a Quaker —

You — son of a bitch —
who triggered the bullets
two to the back
and one to the head
of my brother Chris,
(you hunted him down
like wounded deer,
trailing his bloodtracks
where you pinned his last thoughts
against some scrub oak,
nailed by a .30-caliber rifle
his gaze heavenward)

am a peacemaker, too

will love you for all
the deprived slime you are
shall never understand
how this kind of love
wears my heart
like a curse.

Then the anniversary of Chris's death, September 9, came around. We felt its inevitable arrival with dread and relief. There was nothing to do but "live through" the day.

ANNIVERSARY

And so that day arrives,
A year since the day that stopped us,
Turned us about and upside down
And set us on an unwanted, unplotted

Journey — life without you.

In one breath we say, "Already?" and
"Only one year?"
Time makes us fools —
    It is but a minute since your shining birth;
    Yet the throb of this year has been forever.

How do we mark this day from all the rest?
Avert our hearts with extra tasks?
Surrender to sweet memories and tears?
Regret for a thousandth time the double-cross
Of time and space
That led you to that cursed spot
Where bullets rained?

What *do* we do?

So this is what we did
On that day —
(So like the day you died;
Fluffy clouds sailed in a sky of infinite blue),
We took lunch to the park
By the rose garden,
And there we sat side by side
On a park bench
Musing on your life,
    On you, a truth seeker,
    On you, a sometimes bumbler,
    On you, the earnest one,
    We laughed and cried by turn.
And listened to your songs,
    Dim reflections of you,
    Of your seeking,
    And bumbling,
    And finding.

The first year of life without you
Has passed — so soon — at last.

And we sat on a park bench
By the rose garden,
Hand in hand,
Missing you.

— Reva Griffith, September, 1987

Chapter Twelve

CIRCLES

I'm afraid, I said,
Afraid we'll forget him,
That the memory will die,
That he'll be like a pebble
Flung into a bottomless pond.
The pond shudders
With the splash of the pebble,
Angry rings mark the point of its fall,
Then the circles grow larger
And smoother
And fade . . .
Until the pond's surface
closes once more,
As if the pebble had not fallen.

Will it be that way with him?
Too soon his time here ended,
For him, there are
No more todays and tomorrows,
Only yesterdays grown dim.

My son's friend said,
Fear not, good mother,

His circles have touched us all,
And we've drawn them to us,
Pulled them into our hearts,
Made them part of us,
They are no longer his circles
But ours,
Changing who we are forever.

— Reva Griffith, October, 1987

At the end of the first year, I wrote, "People have said that in the first year most of the heaviness lifts. In our experience, this is true although there are times of crushing sadness. The first anniversary of his death has passed. We are now able to accomplish our tasks with a fair degree of efficiency. Our open grieving has diminished. We carry on 'normally' among our friends and relatives. Most of the time we do the things that constitute 'getting on with our lives.' We love and care about the family that remains. We are involved in worthwhile projects. We enjoy ball games and concerts. We get special joy from our Quaker activities."

We were, though, still "living through" Christopher's death. We were beginning to believe — and in a way this was a relief — that we would probably always be engrossed at some level with just that. We were healing, although we felt as a good friend said regarding her grief at the death of her husband, "I am healing but I'm unwhole."

And again, we found we were not alone in our feelings.

9/15/87 . . . Somehow we have all made it through the first year after Chris's death. People say it gets easier — I wonder if they are right. This year will bring the trial and I also wonder what we will learn about ourselves from that experience — will feelings come up through the scars as raw as they were a year ago? Will it be part of the long lifetime process and another step toward healing?

— A friend of Chris's

10/22/87 ... But I feel Chris around here and I talk to him everyday. I can hear him say, "Grandmommie" just as PLAIN! And I hesitate to do something mean when I think, "Chris wouldn't like that!" And I don't do it. He can NOW be so many places with so many people at one time. ...

— His Grandmommie Griffith

10/88 ... Christopher is with so many people in so many ways and continues to enrich our lives. His ideals for peace and justice are with us more now than ever before. And we work with greater zeal for having known Christopher. ... This, for me, is the "eternal life" symbolized in the Bible, and the way in which we bring more of the "heaven" to our lives and battle the "hell" we must inevitably endure. ...

— One of his best friends

And from Ben, there is another poem written sometime at the end of the first or beginning of the second year after his brother's death.

DEFLECTIONS OF DEATH
for Chris

I dream some device
which deflects those songs
emanating from the land of the dead.
I once again dream/fly
fruitless search for him.

Wavering in the deflections
and those rays which separate
our body's form and soul
In the wake lie my effort

to know, see or understand . . .
flesh of my personality
torn by the melting bombardment —
death sings my own fears.

Friendly words make sense by day.
At night, I fly away to strange places
unable to understand my brother's murder.
— Ben Griffith

And for me, thoughts of Chris still found their way into poetry that autumn.

AUTUMN

Autumn is here,
I walk under a canopy of trees,
Brilliant with color,
Red, yellow, russet;
Intense, blinding, unreal,
All of a piece.

I feel
A quick breath of wind,
I hear
A furtive rustle,
As leaves part from their brothers.

They tumble through the air
Like circus clowns,
Bobbing, floating, diving,
Ever downward,
Until at last
They touch the earth,
Their season done.

And I think of you, my son,
Whose chief delight
In autumn
Was to float down quiet rivers
Lined with brilliance.

You too have fallen, though you,
Unlike leaves whose day has come,
Were torn away before your season,
Reaching earth before your time.
— Reva Griffith, October, 1987

Dreams continued, especially for John. One of the dreams John recorded that year follows (December 12, 1987):

> This morning about 4:00 A.M. I had another dream involving an encounter with Chris. In this dream we were at a large apartment complex — something like a series of dorms at a large university, although it was a complex of regular adult apartments. It seems that I have been at this apartment complex in other dreams. Chris and I were there together, and I was anxious to show Chris where his cousin (Bob Griffith) lived but was unable to remember how to find the apartment.
>
> While the search for this apartment was going on I was aware that Chris was supposed to be dead. He was very real, alive and acted so naturally Chris-like that I found it difficult to figure out how to raise the question with him about his being dead. I was quite anxious about finding the apartment and also understanding how Chris could be with me. Chris, on the other hand, seemed to be free-spirited and without any anxiety. He finally told me not to worry about finding the apartment and he started to play with

> some children. I told Chris that it had been quite awhile since he had last visited us — still not verbalizing the question in my mind about him being dead. Chris responded that it was difficult to visit very often and he said, "Don't worry, Dad, I will come again." The dream ended here. This dream, although having real substance to it, did not have the same intensity of emotional content that previous dreams about Chris had.

John recorded in September, 1988, a story he shared at meeting for worship at Missouri Valley Conference. He told of a near-drowning experience when he was five or six. His father rescued him, jolting him back to life with a spanking.

John writes:

> Although this experience did not seem frightening to me while it was in process, I have since realized that it must have been very frightening to my father. Our perceptions of the event must have been quite different.
>
> This experience has had a continuing influence in my life. I have an intuitive trust that beyond the perplexities of physical accidents, possible death and the unknown, there is a safe haven where things are O.K.
>
> This experience was especially helpful to me two years ago when our son was brutally murdered. From a father's perspective I am haunted by our son's final moments. He was able to run from his assailant — leaving a trail of blood for about one hundred yards — before the fifth bullet brought him to the ground and to his death. And while I do have to live with this, I am greatly comforted with an intuitive insight that those final moments for Chris went much better

> for him than the memory does for me and for those who loved Chris.
>
> (I started this vocal ministry with no difficulty and expected to have no difficulty in articulating what I wanted to share. But when I reached the point of saying "this experience was especially helpful to me two years ago...", the deep anguish a father has experienced over the murder of a son rose up from the depths of my consciousness and it was with difficulty that I finished the rest of this message. I wonder how long it will be before the deep assurance I feel that Chris is O.K. will overcome the pain of losing a beloved son in such a senseless and brutal way?)

We carried on, each in our own way. I raised funds for and edited the newsletter for the local American Friends Service Committee; John performed the duties of clerk of Iowa Yearly Meeting of Friends (Conservative) (analogous to president of the board) and treasurer of Missouri Valley Friends Conference. I started a novel under the guidance of a good writer friend, a novel I considered practice for a real novel although it became real as I progressed. Both John and I performed duties for our beloved Penn Valley Meeting; he as treasurer while I edited the monthly newsletter.

We attended The Compassionate Friends less often that second year. Our need to talk with others who were grieving about their children's deaths was not as great as the first year; yet we weren't ready to play the supportive role to others. In time we realized our relationship to TCF had changed. The rawness of our grief had healed enough that we could listen to the pain of newly bereaved parents and assure them they were not crazy, that we too had suffered their agony in our own way, that sometime, somehow, it would be better, not the same as when their child was alive, but bearable. And perhaps later ... that answer had not yet come.

I don't believe we were really aware when we began to pick up and go on with our lives — we just did it. As we think about it now, we agree that the only other choice was to curl up and retreat into our grief. And although we seldom articulated the thought, we both felt the memory of a tall, hulking, loving Chris beside us, urging us back. We knew he would want us to carry on with our lives; he was pushing us out into the world, ever so gently but firmly.

And while we were grieving the loss of our son, the "wheels of justice" creaked along.

Chapter Thirteen

Then I wish instead
I had been there
To hurl myself between you,
To take the shots he meant for you.

So that you had not fallen
Beside that bridge,
In those woods,
Unsuspecting,
Innocent,
Alone.
from *If Only*... by Reva Griffith, April 1987

A shiver ran through me as I walked with John up the steps of the courthouse in Hillsboro, Missouri late in the afternoon of March 21, 1988. The sun on this chilly early spring day was sinking toward the horizon as it did every other day of the year. The dank odor of spring, usually so exciting with its promise of new growth, was all around, yet how like a chilling nightmare fantasy it seemed for John and me. We were no longer just ordinary people living ordinary lives. I had often seen photos of persons involved in tragedies; now I knew I had not really identified with the human pain that showed there. Today John and I were the people in the pictures. And it was real; we were at this place for the trial of the man who had murdered Chris. He was in jail in that building; we would actually see him the next day.

I thought about how unsuspecting and vulnerable we all are as we live out our lives. I did not believe Donald Reese had intended to be on trial for the murder of our son; we would not have dreamed that Chris would have become one of his victims; and Chris surely had not planned on September 9 to be in the path of bullets from a rifle in the hands of this man he did not know. Sometimes our lives take strange and incongruous turns, sad and irreversible, that change who we are forever. It's almost as if we are actors in a drama, and we haven't been given the lines.

That morning, March 21, John and I had packed enough clothing for a week, and with mingled dread and relief, had driven out of Kansas City, heading down I-70 east toward Columbia, a highway filled with memories of Chris. We approached the Marshall exit, halfway to Columbia, painfully aware that the Marshall Junction Wildlife Area was only a few miles from there. For us it still remained both ugly and sacred, that spot where Chris drew his last breath.

> Griffith's body was found in the woods about 100 yards from the cars. "There was a blood trail leading from the back of the car, as though he tried to run away," patrol Sgt. Watson said.
>
> — *Columbia Daily Tribune*, September 10, 1986

Scattered along the way were restaurants and rest areas where we had paused as we had driven back and forth between Kansas City and Columbia in the sad months following Chris's death; we remembered every one.

As we neared Columbia, we talked, as we probably always will, of how much Chris had liked this town. We stopped for lunch at one of our favorite cafeterias, and memories of days spent in Columbia with Chris crowded into our minds. The steamy June day in 1974 when we helped Chris and Susie, his then wife, move into the house they had rented; Tim, Ben, Chris and John had pushed, shoved and willed a gigantic chest freezer into the basement — we think it may still be there. Times we visited Chris and Susie ticked off in our minds. The numerous houses Chris had lived in there, two of them not far from this cafeteria. The day we hiked in timberland that Chris and some friends had rented so they could have a quiet place for hiking and picnicking; there was a feeling of freedom there as we tramped through grass untouched by the blade of a mower.

The last time we had visited him in the spring of 1986 he had given us the supreme gift of showing us a much-loved spot on a bluff above Gans Creek. Yes, we had visited him in this town he had adopted, although not nearly as often as we wish now.

One of these days
And it won't be long
You'll look for me
And I'll be gone,
Long gone, oh I'll be gone
Long gone, oh I'll be gone.

from *Robert Thomas Blues*
a song by Chris Griffith

At the northeastern edge of Columbia, off to the north of the interstate, almost hidden among the trees, is the funeral home where Chris's body was taken after the shooting. I always look for it, though recalling that day brings pain. It's as if I am compelled to look at places he has been; maybe I hope to catch a glimpse of him there.

From Columbia we traveled on down I-70 to I-55 this side

of St. Louis and veered off to the south. Clouds scudded across the sky as we urged our Toyota toward our destination. It had been a year and a half since the arrest of Donald Reese in the murders of Chris and the other three men at the firing range near Marshall. And while in the midst of our grief, we had seldom given conscious thought to the fate of this man accused of Christopher's murder, the unfinished business of *Missouri* v. *Donald Reese* was stored in our consciousness as something yet to be gone through. We had decided soon after Chris's death and the arrest of Reese that we would go to the trial, that going to the trial of the man who was charged in Chris's murder was another part of taking care of our son.

Preliminary hearings had been held within the first three weeks after the arrest and then the prosecuting attorney in Saline County where the murders occurred had resigned. Taking his place on the case was Tim Finnical, an assistant attorney in the office of the Attorney General of Missouri. We had soon learned that among his peers, Finnical was known as Doctor Death and The Antichrist for his fervent and dramatic prosecution in first degree murder cases. He was an ambitious and busy young man in a state office, and we had found that the best way to get information on what was happening in the case was to call and leave a message at his office for him or someone else to return with any news there might be. John had been doing this from time to time as the months went by.

Finally, about a month before the trial was to take place, we had been informed as to the date and place. Because of the amount and intensity of the publicity surrounding the murders in the Marshall area, both sides had agreed it would be difficult, probably impossible, to get jurors from that area who did not know about the case. So the trial was scheduled for Hillsboro, county seat of Jefferson County, about fifty miles southwest of St. Louis.

In a strategic move, the state would not for this trial charge Reese in the murders of John Burford and Donald Vanderlinden, the brothers-in-law who were murdered first.

Reese was being charged now with murder in the first degree in the deaths of James Watson and Christopher Griffith. Trial on all four deaths at the same time was said to require too much investigation and trial time. And the state was reported to think that there was a clearer case for conviction in the deaths of Watson and Chris. Circumstances cited in Reese's confession made the murders of Watson and Chris seem more cold-blooded and blatant than the deaths of Burford and Vanderlinden. Chris's death seemed the most chilling of all. But in the event conviction was not obtained, Reese could still be charged in the deaths of the other two victims.

The person from Finnical's office who had called us regarding the trial had also informed John that he would be subpoenaed as a witness for the prosecution. We were taken aback because of the first telephone conversation John had had with Tim Finnical after Finnical was assigned the case. "I have been very successful in capital murder cases," Finnical had said, "and I want to assure you that we are going after the death penalty and we are going to get it."

To which John replied, "I think you ought to know that my wife and I are opposed to the death penalty. If we should be called as witnesses, and if we should be asked about our feelings about the death penalty, we would tell of our opposition to capital punishment."

Finnical then said that it would be unlikely that he would call us as witnesses and the defense would certainly not have any reason to do so. John also told him that in deference to the other families who might not agree with us, we had decided not to talk publicly about our feelings on this issue until after the trial.

At about 3:00 P.M., March 21, we had pulled into Gannon's Best Western Motel in Festus, Missouri. Festus, located eight miles east of Hillsboro, is a small Missouri town on the interstate highway with more to offer in motel and restaurant accommodations than Hillsboro's one small motel and two downtown restaurants. The state had arranged for victims' families to be housed on the third floor of Gannon's. In the elevator, we spoke with two women attired in pants and jackets who looked as though they might be sisters. We had wondered if they could be the wives of Burford and Vanderlinden, the brothers-in-law who were murdered first. Both short, they spoke to us in a friendly manner. Later we discovered they were indeed Mrs. Burford and Mrs. Vanderlinden.

Our room seemed spacious; our usual home away from home is of Motel 6 variety. Since Bob and Ann (John's brother and his wife, who had asked to be there with us) hadn't arrived yet, we decided to drive over to Hillsboro to see where the courthouse was and to determine what had happened so far. The road from Festus to Hillsboro wound through hills reminiscent of the foothills of the Blue Ridge. The courthouse, a square brick building, was located at the top of a sizable hill; yes, the town was properly named. We parked in the lot behind the courthouse and walked uphill and into the courthouse. We were told in the Clerk of Court's office that jury selection was slow and would undoubtedly go on into the next day. We found that John, as a subpoenaed witness, could not observe what went on in the courtroom, including jury selection.

We walked out of the courthouse to our car, sharing our mixed-up feelings over the trial. We wanted it to be over; yet we dreaded the pain that we knew would come as the trial proceeded through the inevitable revelations of the circumstances of Chris's death.

Bob and Ann were at the motel when we returned. We were very grateful they had come. Our three living sons were involved in their own occupations, and while we would have welcomed them if they had been able to come, we felt it was important for them, with families of their own, to suffer as little disruption as possible in their lives. There had already been plenty of that with Christopher's death. So, Bob and Ann, also retired, furnished the supportive family ingredient for us. On cue, we were greeted with smiles and much-needed hugs.

The next morning in the hallway of the motel we met Tim Finnical, the prosecuting attorney, an imposing young man with reddish hair and glasses. He was friendly, though detached. He told us John was free to sit in the courtroom; he had decided not to use him as a witness. (We were relieved and certainly not surprised.) Finnical also told us that the whole day would be taken up with jury selection.

The four of us decided to go to the courtroom and watch the selection process. We drove over to Hillsboro where we took the elevator to the second floor and made our way to the courtroom. I would need to go back to the courtroom to describe it. I can only feel it as I think about it now. It did not seem forbidding to me. The room was well-lit and the benches where observers sat were of light wood. We had ample choice of where to sit since there were few observers; we chose a third row bench toward the mid-left of the room. The benches, while hard, had a comfortable shape.

As I sat there looking about the room, I felt this thing, this unfinished burden of what was to happen to the man who murdered Chris, was temporarily out of our hands and in the hands of others.

Over 110 jurors had been called, and the day before been reduced by 38. Some knew about the murders; others were hardship cases. The remaining 80 came into the courtroom in panels of 11–18; each group was examined by the prosecution and then the defense.

"Do you have any moral, ethical or religious principles such that you would not be able if a person is found guilty of murder in the first degree, committed after deliberate and cool reflection, to impose the death penalty?" And then, "Can you conceive likewise of any circumstance in which you would not be able to impose life imprisonment without possibility of probation or parole?" These two questions were asked by the prosecution of each prospective juror.

In Missouri, anyone who either automatically supports the death penalty for first-degree murder or could never consider capital punishment is excluded from serving on the jury in a first-degree murder case.

The defense then labored through informing and probing as each prospective juror was educated on aggravating and mitigating circumstances. As I understand it, aggravating circumstances indicate criminal intent while mitigating circumstances explain behavior on bases other than criminal intent. According to Missouri law, the aggravating circumstances must outweigh the mitigating circumstances if a person is to be convicted of first-degree murder. Linda Murphy, the defense attorney who questioned the jurors, urged them not to presume guilt; Reese was to be presumed innocent until proven guilty.

I wish I could describe some of the jurors. I see them now much as an impressionistic painting. They looked like the people on the streets of Hillsboro — mostly rural, mostly not college-educated, white, old and young, men and women. I know each one was distinctive in his or her own right and I want to record that I saw that; I just can't remember specific people. I was impressed by their general ability to understand the questions and by what I perceived as honesty in answering these questions. John especially remembers the man who said he didn't believe in the death penalty but he didn't know how he'd feel if a member of his family was murdered. John, Bob, Ann and I were surprised at the thoughtfulness of most of the respondents as they attempted to discern and express their true feelings.

By 8:15 P.M., after a full, mostly uninterrupted day of questions and answers, a jury of twelve men and women, and two alternates, was selected by a process we didn't quite understand, although it involved "give and take" on the part of prosecution and defense attorneys. We went back to the motel, exhausted but impressed.

And what was my reaction to the defendant, Donald Edward Reese? He sat all day in the front of the courtroom. Wearing a long-sleeved shirt stretched over a small pot belly, and a pair of wash pants, he looked much like the picture I had seen in the paper except he was shorter than I had envisioned. "Smaller than life," I thought. The slant of his eyes made me wonder whether he was retarded (later I dismissed that idea). I thought, "If I met him on the street, I would hardly notice him." Strange that he did not appear to be the epitome of evil. That thought brought me up short for I could not forget that his evil deed had taken a dear son's life.

Most of the time Reese stared straight ahead, not moving a muscle. In one of his infrequent glances at the people in the courtroom, I thought his eyes (now he looked more like the enemy) met mine and then quickly shifted away. Did he guess who I was? I wondered what he was thinking. Was he sorry for what he had done? Or did he in some convoluted way blame us for Chris's being in his path that day?

And what were my feelings as our eyes met? From the time we arrived in Hillsboro the night before, and even before that, I had been afraid of these very feelings. Now Donald Edward Reese, a living, breathing being, not an idea, was before me. It would have been dramatic to feel hate flare, and distressing to know what to do with it; it would have been soothing to feel a wave of forgiveness, though I had been unable most of the time to associate Chris's death with the act of a person. The fact that Chris was dead had been the all-consuming concern, and it still was. In truth, as I looked at Donald Reese, I was not aware of strong feelings of any kind. Again, it was almost as if I were viewing an actor in a play.

The trial was set to begin.

Chapter Fourteen

Christopher Griffith
July 25, 1948 – September 9, 1986

> He truly tried to live his days in an attitude of caring for those about him, constantly searching for the truth in all things, both in his personal life and in the world. It was perhaps his willingness always to talk and to enter into another's suffering that will be missed most. His untimely departure from this life leaves a gaping hole in the hearts of family, friends and patients.
>
> — from the obituary read at the memorial service in Columbia held September 13, 1986:

The next morning at 9:00 A.M., Donald Edward Reese, handcuffed, wearing a white shirt, expressionless, was escorted into the courtroom. Everyone stood as the jury entered the box and the judge came into the room.

Then the bailiff, a middle-aged man with a smile that never ceased, intoned, "Hear ye, hear ye, the Circuit Court of Jefferson County is now in session. Judge John L. Anderson presiding. Please be seated and be in order, Thank you."

As one, we sat down.

On a platform above us, behind a large desk-like structure

(as in the movies), sat the judge, Circuit Court Judge John Anderson, attired in black robe. He was a pleasant looking man, probably in his early fifties. I wondered how he would play his part in this drama. To his right, facing him, was the table where the prosecution sat; prosecuting attorneys were Tim Finnical, and Chip Perry, Lafayette County prosecuting attorney. To the judge's left at a similar table were public defenders, Mark Kempton from Concordia, and the only woman among the principal players, Linda Murphy, St. Louis. Seated also at that table was the defendant.

The jury, five men and seven women, were in assigned seats in armchairs in "the box" at the far right of the judge. The alternates, a man and a woman, were seated to their left.

To complete the courtroom scene, observers occupied benches facing the judge. There must have been seven or eight rows of benches with three benches across. In these seats were family members and friends of the victims and the defendant, reporters, and the curious. There were even some fans of Tim Finnical, the prosecuting attorney; we spoke with one of them, a retired man who enjoyed Finnical's histrionics so much that he followed him from case to case when he was able.

We had by this time met most of the families of the other victims. Children of Mr. Watson sat together over to the left and close to the front, near the jury. These included his son, a tall, dark young man, and the son's wife, and two willowy well-dressed daughters, both of whom worked at KU Medical Center in Kansas City. All of them were in their middle to late twenties. James Watson's wife was not present since she was to testify later. Also absent were the wives of Donald Vanderlinden and John Burford since they too had been subpoenaed; other members of their families were there.

To our right and near the back of the courtroom was Donald Reese's mother, a slight, fragile, elderly woman with a stoop. Her hair was pulled back into a knot in the back revealing a sorrowful face. She was dressed neatly but not in the latest fashion; she reminded me of the woman in Grant Wood's *American Gothic*. A good-looking woman, Reese's sister, blonde, stylishly attired, sat beside her; we heard later that she lived in Florida and had come to be with her mother during the trial. From time to time other family members were present at the trial; some of them too were excluded because of future testimony.

The opening argument for the prosecution was presented by Chip Perry, the assistant attorney in the case. An energetic, nearly bald young man with a serious, aggressive demeanor, he concentrated on Reese's confession of the murders and his having taken money from billfolds of three of the victims. "... the very same day of the killings, he began paying off in cash, delinquent debts ..." He also emphasized the brutality of the killings.

The opening statement of the defense countered that Reese was set up for an arrest. In an effort to gain sympathy for the defendant, Mark Kempton, defense attorney, said, "You will see that Donald Reese is not very intelligent. He's a hard worker, but not too smart. He was made-to-order for this investigation." Kempton, acting as public defender, small and blond, was soft-spoken and controlled. In contrast, his partner, Linda Murphy, a plumpish woman who was attentive to "Eddie", as she called the defendant, was sometimes abrasive.

> "Do you swear to tell the truth, the whole truth, and nothing but the truth, so help you God?"
>
> "I do."
>
> The witness, a man who had been driving near the rifle range late in the afternoon of September 9, took his seat on the stand. A truck driver who had come forth as a witness, he sat twisting his hands as he waited.
>
> The prosecuting attorney stood before him.

"Can you tell us what you saw September 9 as you drove down the county road toward the Interstate?"

"I saw a light-colored '75–'78 Buick coming up behind me at a high rate of speed."

"How did you know the car was traveling at a high rate of speed?"

"Because of the dust it was kicking up and the distance it was covering."

"How did you know what kind of car it was?"

"I have a '77 Buick with a front end like that."

As the trial started, I took notes. However, it wasn't long until I realized I didn't want to be tied to my notebook and only jotted down a few notes from time to time. The testimony above, taken from these notes, is only a facsimile of actual testimony in the trial on Wednesday, March 23. We had hoped to get a transcript of the trial but found it would be very expensive; this story of the trial is based on newspaper clippings, notes and memory. During the trial, more than twenty witnesses testified for the prosecution; these included several lawmen, the truck driver mentioned above, a conservation agent, Reese's former boss, the Boone County medical examiner, the physician who performed the autopsies, a man who sold Reese a used car after the shootings, wives of the three other victims, called to identify their husbands' wallets and to corroborate the amount of money they had carried. The witnesses were questioned by the prosecution and cross-examined by the defense.

The prosecution was led by Tim Finnical. Of medium build and in his late thirties, he lived up to his billing of vigorous prosecution in first-degree murder trials. With thick, wavy auburn hair and a redhead's complexion, his face would flush, his coat be discarded, his tie loosened, as he paced in front of the jury, trying to make a point. Often he used graphic details and dramatization to emphasize the horrible aspects of the crime. Sometimes his glasses would creep down on his nose and his voice would rise as he strode back and forth. His presence was indeed attention-getting.

Crucial evidence included a five-page confession dictated by Reese (the day after his arrest) to Sheriff Darnell of Lafayette County. Sheriff Darnell led the investigation of the killings. A paragraph from the *Columbia Daily Tribune* of March 25 read, "Darnell testified yesterday that before confessing, Reese had been read his rights twice, signed two rights-waiver forms and had had his rights explained to him." However, because of an apparent lack of communication among the authorities, Reese had, before the confession and unknown to Darnell, filled out a third form making specific request for a lawyer for the upcoming hearing. At a preliminary hearing months before, it had been ruled that this confession could be allowed in spite of the slip-up.

Other evidence included wallets, over $2,000, and a .30-caliber rifle, all found at sites specified by Reese; .30-caliber shells found at the scene of the murder; a .30-caliber shell found under the hood of Reese's car; one package of Marlboro cigarettes found at the firing range and another partial pack at one of the sites where Reese led law officers, plus an alleged admission by Reese that he smoked Marlboros; photos of the victims showing multiple wounds caused by a high powered weapon; testimony from the medical examiner and physician as to cause of death of the victims.

> (I remember the young Chris and toy guns. In the early days of TV when he was seven or eight, he was in love with cowboys. He had a ritual where he would leap onto his horse — the arm of the big chair in the living room — ride out onto the prairie and shoot at the bad guys. A few months later the game was over; that was the end of guns for him. Until his death!)

The trial began Wednesday; mid-afternoon Friday Tim Finnical for the prosecution rather abruptly rested his case.

In a forty-minute defense, Reese was portrayed as the victim of an investigation that was going nowhere. The jury was told, "The whole state of Missouri — the Missouri State Highway Patrol, deputies, police lab technicians — are a formidable force against Ed Reese."

Throughout the trial, the defense relied on vigorous cross-examination of witnesses for the prosecution. It was obvious they were trying to create doubt in the minds of the jury as to the validity of the confession as well as to hammer away at the "need of a victim" theory. There were frequent objections during the trial, especially by the defense, probably to establish cause for an appeal if needed. Objections were sometimes loudly contested; numerous conferences which took place between the judge and attorneys made it necessary for the court reporter, a blonde woman, lithe and young, to leave her seat in front of the judge's desk and carry her equipment to wherever the conference was to occur.

The judge was always in control. Sometimes as he sat above us in his black robe and leaned back in his chair, he glanced about the courtroom, his reading glasses propped on his nose, seemingly inattentive to what was happening. Yet when there was an objection raised, he was ready to make a decision. Sometimes I thought he looked at the four of us, especially when the manner of Chris's death was described. I remember deciding I would not cry and I didn't, although tears gathered in the corners of my eyes and my mouth trembled. At one recess, the Watson young people were advised by the prosecution not to display their emotions so much and were asked to move to a seat where they would not be so visible to the jury. We understand that the word had come down from the judge that obvious and noisy grief might be construed as an effort to influence the jury and could result in a mistrial.

Following that particular recess, we returned to the

courtroom and found the Watsons ensconced in the seat we had established as ours. When they saw us, they apologized profusely for taking our seat, but they didn't move. We tried to find a seat that suited us as well, although we never felt quite as comfortable elsewhere.

After the prosecution and defense had presented their evidence, the judge declared a recess while he prepared instructions for the jury; an hour later court reconvened and he read the instructions, well laid out, clear and concise, as to what was expected of the jury. For the first time, they knew which two murders were being prosecuted.

Then the defense did a quiet but effective summation, discrediting evidence and witnesses, building a case of a man distraught with his wife's leaving him for another man, caught in a web of circumstantial evidence by law enforcement officers who needed to arrest someone for a heinous crime. Kempton told the jury, "There is not one piece of evidence that puts that man on the scene."

Finnical demonstrated his fire-and-brimstone technique in the closing statement for the prosecution. He shouted, "Ed Reese is the man who murdered these people. The motive for the crime was clearly robbery. Some of America's best, murdered by what has turned out to be America's worst. He killed them because he's greedy, because he's mean." Noting Chris's death, he said, "You shoot somebody five times in the back, you've deliberated." And later, he said "they didn't have a chance." These were not easy things to hear; at times it was almost as if we were witnessing Chris's very death in the courtroom. Sometimes I thought I could stand to hear no more.

The jury (now six men and six women since one woman had been replaced upon her revelation that after the trial started she realized she was familiar with the case) left the courtroom around 7:00 P.M. to deliberate the verdict.

The rest of the actors — attorneys, witnesses, families of the victims and defendant, the smiling bailiff and the clerks, reporters, interested persons, milled about the building. Hardly anyone left the building lest they miss the dramatic conclusion of the hours spent in the courtroom. Most either sent an emissary to a restaurant or relied on junk food from the snack machines for the evening meal.

At this point, it seemed that the prosecution had clearly established Reese's guilt. Shortly before 11:00 P.M., the word quickly passed that a verdict had been reached and we all hurried to the courtroom and found seats. The jurors, impassive of countenance, came in and took their places; the judge handed the verdict to the clerk of court to read.

And she read, "On count one, we the jury find the defendant, Donald Edward Reese, guilty of murder in the first degree." The same words were read for count two. Finnical and Perry looked at one another, allowing themselves a smile at last. Phase two, jury recommendation of the sentence, death or life imprisonment without chance of probation or parole, would take place the next day.

(Guilty. An empty word. Guilty won't bring Chris back. I suppose I am glad for the verdict. There is some solace in knowing the man who did this thing will not be free. Still, Chris is gone.)

As the four of us went outside into the night air, we heaved a collective sigh of relief that the first, and the most difficult, part of the trial was over. On the way back to the motel, Bob and Ann told us they would need to leave early in the morning. Their oldest son and his family were coming to visit them and they needed to get back to get ready for their arrival. Their presence for those days was a gift beyond compare. We told them good-bye before we parted for the evening. I don't think they realized just how comforting it had been to have them with us. Going out with them to meals in Hillsboro had been an adventure; there was good conversation to distract from the pain of the trial. In the evenings there were quiet visits at the motel as we talked of many things close to us all. We missed them the next day.

The next day, March 26, 1988, the *Kansas City Times* headline read: GUILTY VERDICT RETURNED IN WILDLIFE AREA SLAYINGS.

Saturday morning at 10:00 A.M., we gathered once more in the courtroom. By now the actors and the scripts were familiar: the fiery prosecutors, the canny defenders, the defendant with the blank stare, and the rest of us, many of us unwilling participants in a drama that had brought us pain and changed our lives.

The prosecution introduced two new witnesses. One of these, a relative who had attended the double funeral of Vanderlinden and Burford testified that Reese was at the funeral viewing the bodies, that when he saw Reese's picture on TV after his arrest he remembered him because "he was wearing the same shirt as at the funeral; it was a western-style shirt with a monogram." A spooky testimony.

The other witness was a young man who had been a cellmate of Reese in the Saline County jail the August after the murders. Because the young man had claimed paralegal knowledge, Reese had told him about the murders. Linda Murphy (for the defense) tried to discredit his testimony claiming he might have benefitted his own case by telling about Reese. When she asked why he told the sheriff about this conversation, he replied, "Because he (Reese) scared the hell out of me!"

The defense, attempting to build a case for life imprisonment, called several witnesses. One was a Marshall physician who testified he prescribed Librium for Reese for his nerves the day before the shootings; then there was a pharmacologist who testified Librium could cause a paradoxical (unexpected) reaction in some persons.

In addition, friends and family members testified as to the character of Reese. Their stories presented him as a hapless victim of poverty who had financial and marital problems, a Christian who played the guitar with a gospel music group made up of his friends. A sister testified that when Reese was a child, their father, an alcoholic, abused him. Donald Reese was never called to testify in his own behalf. In an interview while the verdict was being decided, he said, "I wish they would have let me get up on the stand . . . I want to get up on the stand today," adding that she, Linda Murphy, "said she don't want me to."

The prosecution made its closing statement, going over once more the horror of it all, arguing the weakness of the mitigating circumstances. Chip Perry asked for the death penalty, saying, "Sympathy and mercy should have no place in this courtroom today . . . There was no mercy or sympathy on September 9, 1986."

The defense, leaning on the possibility that the drug had affected Reese's personality, and on the caring of his family, said, ". . . Doesn't forty-four years of a good life count for something?" Murphy declared that in a sense Reese is already dead. "Look at him. You've seen him here in the courtroom this week. He's only a shell of a man."

In the final statement of the prosecution, Finnical was again impassioned. No remorse had been expressed by the defendant; the lives of the victims have ended, there is no more for them; why should there be more life for him?

(I wonder if Donald Reese is sorry. It might help if he'd just say he's sorry. But even if he should say he's sorry, I don't believe the picture of the dying Chris will ever be erased from my mind. Can I forgive?)

At 6:00 P.M., the jury again retired to deliberate. With the others, we roamed dim halls of the courthouse, snacking from the machines. As the hours dragged on, John and I reflected that the chances of a life imprisonment verdict might increase with the length of time it took to decide.

During the time of deliberation, a reporter for the *Columbia Daily Tribune* whom we had told of our opposition to the death penalty interviewed us. We decided it was time to talk about our feelings. John was quoted in the paper as saying, "Our personal way of looking at life is just as Chris believed: violence never solves problems. . . . When the state kills someone, it is perpetuating the illusion that killing a human being is a proper basis for solving problems."

When the prosecution and defense found out about the interview, both said our views could have affected the outcome as the jury recommended the sentence. We still feel it was right to withhold our personal opinions until the people of Missouri, through the jury system, had spoken. Also, knowing how at least one of the other families viewed the matter convinced us it was right to let that part of the process take its course.

At 1:00 A.M. Sunday, the jury returned to the courtroom with a recommendation — death. We were not surprised.

As the verdict was read on both counts, Reese hardly moved a muscle. His face maintained the same vacant expression it had had all week. His family cried and left the room. Then the courtroom was silent. It was obvious that everyone knew this was a serious matter. Even those who were "victorious" were subdued.

We went back to the motel, feeling sick. By chance, we rode up to our floor with the Watson family who were elated with the verdict. By this time, they knew how we viewed the death penalty. One of the daughters with whom I had spoken earlier, looked at me with sympathy and said, "Are you all right?"

So we went to bed, got up a few hours later, had breakfast and started home. Instead of going back by the interstate, we took picturesque Route 94 on the north side of the Missouri

River to Jefferson City. We needed the beauty and tranquillity of the countryside, the majesty of the bluffs along the river, glimpses of the river going its way with ponderous peace. Our hearts and minds were not at rest. A man had been sentenced to die for Chris's death, thereby adding to the suffering his mad act had already caused. We felt reasonably sure that Chris, if he had been the one faced with a family death, would have felt as we did — that capital punishment will breed more pain in a situation already loaded with pain. We felt we would need to keep our minds open to trying to make a difference in Missouri law regarding the death penalty. While this notion may seem like blind heroism to some and foolishness to others, it comes from years of exposure to Quaker principles.

As I look back at all the places of that week — the courtroom, the motel, the towns — they seem like pieces of a stage set in a week of drama. Even the restaurants of my memory are sets for a play. Those in Hillsboro, an old Missouri town back from the highway, were small and quaint. The influx of folks coming to a murder trial stretched their capacity, so that for noon meals the booths and tables were crowded. The food, served with friendly flair, was generally home-cooked — meat, potatoes with lots of gravy, pie. Meals in Festus were like those along any interstate in the country.

The feeling of being taken care of came to me in the courtroom. Even now, four years later, I feel protected. In the motel, there was a certain grim but caring camaraderie among those of us involved in the trial. Families of the victims were looked upon with sympathy; we did sense a subtle change on the part of some people as our view on the death penalty became known. Although we were invited to the victory celebration on the third floor of Gannon's, we did not attend. We didn't feel like celebrating.

The court process was impressive. Things got done with deliberate fairness. Even though the prosecuting attorneys may have viewed us with some anxiety, they treated us with consideration. The defense attorneys were noteworthy; he for the sharpness of his argument, she for her compassion for the accused. Law enforcement officers couldn't have been more thoughtful. The jury, those silent nameless folks charged with deciding a man's fate, were crucial actors in the drama, actors we never knew except as they sat attentively day after day, their eyes glued to the witness stand, being fed bits and pieces upon which they were to deliberate to make a life-threatening decision.

People we recognized as reporters with their pads and pencils, computers and questions came and went from the scene, as did others, some of them friends of ours and of other families of victims and the defendant.

There was a community of pain among the families of victims. Although it was clear we had reacted to the deaths of our loved ones differently, we all had suffered and we empathized with one another. For some, there was religious acceptance (it was God's will); for others, a getting on with life; for still others, a day-to-day living with the death. For all, there was lingering pain and deep regret. I'm sure we all saw this in one another.

And then there was the family of Donald Edward Reese. Mrs. Reese (Reese's mother) fell coming out of a restaurant and broke her hip on the second day. A fragile woman, she was taken to the hospital and was never able to return to the trial. Ann spoke with her daughter the day of the accident and told her she was sorry about her mother's injury. That gave me courage to talk with the woman about her mother and her injury and about the other, deeper pain the Reese family was suffering. Her eyes filled with tears as she said, "I know my mother would want you to know how sorry we are about your son."

One of Reese's best friends, a musician, went to all the families of the victims and expressed sorrow for what had happened to the four men. At the time the jury was to recommend a sentence, a silent, pretty, blonde woman, Reese's estranged wife we believe, sat with a young boy, probably one of his sons. The sadness in her face cannot be described.

And to those who may question why we went to the trial and reopened the pain (not quite accurate since it was there all the time), this is the explanation I wrote to our family: "You may wonder why we put ourselves through all this when we didn't have to. It's all a part of seeing the earthly existence of dear Chris through to the end. . . . The memory of Chris is always with us; and while being reminded this way is painful, still it is of Chris, and a memory, no matter how painful, is part of living out this horrible thing that happened to him. He is gone, but we are still here to represent him in whatever way we can." True to this day.

The next step was the sentencing of Reese to take place at Hillsboro May 5.

Chapter Fifteen

WHOSE RIGHT?

Death, the jury had said,
The man, they said, should die.

In the courtroom,
Between the heads,
I looked at the man,
(I had thought I couldn't),
He sat unmoving,
Staring ahead,
Face set in a mask.

I thought:
Why did you do it?
Why did you kill him
and the others?
Why?
Who gave you the right?

I thought:
Turn around,
Look at me,
See my sorrow,
See my pain.

Still he sat
Staring, staring,
Catatonic;
Lost in a maze.
A creature of the universe,
As my son had been.

And they said he should die,
Who gave them the right?
— Reva Griffith, May, 1988

In the weeks between the trial in late March and the scheduled sentencing in May, John and I wrote a letter to Judge Anderson. Actually, John masterminded this effort. He had studied the death penalty issue more carefully than I, although we both had strong feelings against it. We both also felt Chris would not have wanted someone put to death for his murder, even a man who was clearly guilty. John drafted a letter; then we thought about it and talked about it, revised it, and finally mailed it to the judge on April 20.

We asked that he pass the lesser of the two sentences for Chris's murder; we said we did not doubt that Reese murdered our son and the other men; we stated that putting Mr. Reese to death "is adding to the needless violence in our society and is nurturing the illusion which already afflicts our society that killing people can be justified and that killing solves problems."

Then we concluded, "We realize that, after the jury has recommended the death penalty, it would require a great deal of courage to pass the lesser of the two available sentences for Mr. Reese. We are aware that, in their terrible grief, some other family members of the murdered men may feel that Mr. Reese should be put to death. Nevertheless, we feel we must express our feeling that the death penalty only compounds the violence in our society.

"We appeal to you not to sentence Mr. Reese to death for the murder of our son."

We did not mount a campaign for others to write the judge. However, our own Friends meeting in Kansas City, Penn Valley Meeting, sent a letter to Judge Anderson, and we were grateful. The following words come from that letter: "In September 1986, the members of Penn Valley Meeting of Friends were horrified to learn of the murder of Christopher Griffith, son of our dear friends, John and Reva Griffith, and of three other men. We were saddened by the suffering of Chris's family and friends. We were disheartened that violence had taken a useful and peace-loving man from the world and had burdened the lives of people who cared for him. . . .

"We agree that society must protect itself from individuals who, like Donald Reese, have shown they cannot be trusted not to kill. We also recognize that society may require some measure of punishment and deterrence. Nevertheless, we believe we have no right to kill another sentient human being; we believe we cannot end violence by participating in it."

Columbia Meeting also inquired if they might write to Judge Anderson and we said yes. The Columbia Meeting letter read in part: ". . . We write because of our own opposition to the taking of human life, which is part of Quaker tradition, and because Chris Griffith, although not a regular attender at our Meeting, was a valued friend of many members and fully shared our concerns about nonviolence and the need to work for a friendlier and more compassionate world. Far better than most of us, he was able to project his beliefs into concrete action to help others. . . . In memory of Chris and his philosophy of nonviolence and of his vision of a better world, we express the hope that the death penalty will not be imposed."

We were told other individuals in Columbia wrote letters expressing the feeling that it would be a disservice to Chris to execute someone for his death. We were pleased for the support of Friends and of friends of Christopher.

While we were not optimistic that the efforts to influence

the sentencing would be successful, we felt we had to try; the support of others lifted our hopes. The media and the prosecution had referred to the killings in such terms as "mass murder" and "massacre"; it would take a gutsy judge to go against the jury's recommendation.

So we wrote our letter and waited for the time of sentencing of Donald Edward Reese.

On May 1, we attended the Second Annual Christopher Griffith Memorial Run/Walk/Bike Event.

A friend from Columbia sent a clipping from the *Columbia Daily Tribune* of April 18, 1988. Forrest Rose, a columnist, had written a feature article on the upcoming event. He wrote, "... I'm now in training for an athletic event that signifies far more than who can run fastest or jump highest. The Second Annual Christopher Griffith Memorial Run/Walk/Bike Event will pay tribute to a man who dedicated his short life to helping those who could neither run, walk nor bicycle." He then reflected on the soon-to-be sentencing of Reese, "I sincerely believe that the legacy Chris would least like to leave would be the sacrifice of another human life, even his slayer's. The memorial run, in contrast, is an affirmation of life of which he would have heartily approved."

The event was a wonderful, bittersweet experience for us. It was uplifting to see the crowd that gathered; 120 actually took to the road. It was sad to reflect on how much Chris would have enjoyed the event; yet here we were memorializing him.

The atmosphere was non-competitive and friendly. Unlike the year before, it was sunny and warm. John and I walked with friends up and down the rolling hills that make Columbia such a pretty little city, through the aisle of trees that hover over a specially constructed walkway. The combination of a beautiful countryside and the easy camaraderie made all of us winners. After four and a half miles I felt my game knee crunch; I decided valor was not called for in this case and caught a ride in one of the cars cruising the route to pick up drop-outs. To Chris, I silently said, "I really tried to finish, but I just couldn't. I'm sorry I had to quit." And I felt his answer, "Mom, you didn't quit; I'm proud you walked as far as you did." John finished the course — eight miles — and won a special plaque as the oldest finisher.

WOUNDED TIGER

"And what is your reaction to this event?"
A microphone is in my face.

I look about me . . .
Lithe young girls somersault over one another on
   blue mats;
Small children play with boats in a yellow plastic pool;
Happy music fills the air;
Triumphant runners, bikers, walkers cross the finish
   line
Amid cheers;
Those who have already finished — the object is to
   finish, not win — relax and munch goodies in the
   sun;
Red, blue, yellow balloons float skyward;

It is the Christopher Griffith 2nd Annual Memorial
Run/Walk/Bike Event.

I had, moments before, thought how Chris would
have liked this event;
(It was almost as if he had planned it);
The simplicity, the good cheer, the song, the children;
I imagined him gamboling about like a happy, dancing bear, mingling with his old friends, making
new ones.
I decided then if anyone asked me how I felt about it,
I would smile and say, "Chris would have liked
this."
Now I look at the pleasant young woman, poised,
microphone in hand,
And I say, willing the smile, "I was only a few moments ago thinking how much . . . Chris . . ."
The smile breaks; tears splash from my eyes.
"Oh, I didn't mean . . ." she says, her smile fading.

It is peculiar — this grief —
It hides behind smiles, words, ready to spring out like
a wounded tiger.

— Reva Griffith, May 1988

On the afternoon of May 4 we once again began the long trek from Kansas City down Interstate 70 toward St. Louis, a route that had become hauntingly familiar. We were on our way to Hillsboro where the formal sentencing of Donald Edward Reese, the man convicted of murdering Chris, would take place.

Again we stopped at Festus to find our motel. This time, on our own money rather than the state's, we settled in at the Drury Inn for the night. The next morning, with a strange and incongruous feeling of having come home, we drove over to Hillsboro, hardly aware of the day, although I believe the sun was shining. We found our way to the courtroom once more where we took possession of *our* bench.

We noticed many of the same people milling about in the courtroom before court convened — the attorneys, the clerk of court, the court reporter, the bailiff, and others. We didn't see the families of the other victims. And Donald Reese's mother, that sad, quiet little woman, was not there.

The defense attorney, Mark Kempton, who had spoken with John several times by telephone, brought us a statement concerning John's allegation that he had told Tim Finnical, the prosecuting attorney, about our death penalty sentiments. Kempton said Finnical had agreed it was true and Kempton wanted John's verification of the statement he had written. He told us the judge had received several letters asking for the lesser of the two sentences for Reese. Kempton wanted to know if John would want to testify as to his views. John asked Kempton if he thought it would make any difference if he testified and Kempton said he didn't know. So we asked him if we could talk it over for a few minutes.

Kempton came back almost immediately and asked us, his face inscrutable, to step out into the hall. Still looking as if he were talking over the back fence, he said the judge had just told him he was going to give Reese life imprisonment in Chris's death so it was not necessary for John to testify unless he particularly wanted to. Although John was prepared to testify, it seemed redundant for him to do so with this knowledge. Now, as I look back, I wish John had testified anyway. He was prepared and his testimony written into the court record would have been articulate and moving. It also might have made John feel he had done something positive in the face of the incredible pain we had suffered.

So, lifted by the promise of a life sentence in Chris's case, we once more took our seats. It felt strange to be associating with the defense, sort of like fraternizing with the enemy. The prosecuting attorney barely acknowledged our presence; I suppose he realized our actions might tarnish his death penalty record.

Then came the familiar call from the smiling bailiff, "Hear ye, hear ye, hear ye, the Circuit Court of Jefferson County is now in session. Judge John L. Anderson presiding. Please be seated and be in order."

Later, we obtained a transcript of the sentencing portion of the trial. Quotations from Judge Anderson and Donald Reese are taken from that transcript.

The first orders of business were motions by the defense for a new trial, acquittal, and for reduction of sentences on both counts. Part of the consideration on these motions was the prior knowledge of the prosecution of our views on the death penalty, the defense contending this should have been presented as a "mitigating factor." After hearing both attorneys, the judge ruled against the motion for a new trial and acquittal. On the reduction of sentence, he overruled in respect to Count 1 (Mr. Watson) and said he would address the motion with regard to Count 2 (Chris).

Then Donald Edward Reese, looking a bit thinner than before, this time wearing a suit, was sworn in and the judge proceeded with the sentencing. He informed the defendant and the rest of the courtroom that different sentences would be imposed on each count.

He said, "The jury's recommendation on both was death. ... That is a choice that the body politic of this State has a right to make. It is an appropriate political and social decision. Like all organic and statutory law, it carries with it the morality that is the consent for the governed. Reasonable men and women may differ over the efficacy of the choice that has been made.

"It is not for the judge to substitute his personal beliefs and, in effect, repeal the law. That, of course, would be a gross usurpation of power in this Court. The judge can never be civilly disobedient. If he cannot discharge the law, he can resign."

He went on to say that due process had been followed in regard to Reese's trial. The jury had conscientiously discharged their duty and recommended death on both counts.

"... A judge should not depart from their recommendation except where the most cogent of reasons exists. ...

"In the case of Christopher Griffith, there are reasons for departing. This Court has always been highly cognizant of the rights of victims and the suffering of victims. Of course, the judge can never substitute the desires of the victim for his own consideration, and hopefully, unemotional and impartial judgment. However, victims' rights and consideration of the victims forms part of the dynamic of the decision-making process.

"Christopher Griffith and his parents had and have convictions concerning the death penalty that are very profound, very real and genuine. ... To sentence Donald Edward Reese to death in this murder of Christopher Griffith, I think, would do injury to his parents and those who loved him and those who worked with him with regard to the death penalty and his feelings about violence.

"I very much appreciate the letter from Mr. and Mrs. Griffith that I received in this matter, as well as the recommendations that I received from the religious Friends Society in Columbia and various other friends of Christopher Griffith.

"It may seem a little strange that I would reduce the sentence in this Griffith case and not in the Watson case, but I don't feel I can do it in both. I think, perhaps, Christopher Griffith would prefer that I did it in both, but I'm not going to do that.

"The Court is going to impose death in Count 1, but the Court is going to impose life imprisonment without parole with regard to Count 2." The judge read his statement in a firm voice, looking up from his text now and then and over the top of his reading glasses at the courtroom. It seemed a remarkably sincere and courageous act on his part. The courtroom was silent.

Then the defendant was asked if he had anything to say. After some hesitation, he replied in a low voice, "All I can say is I'm not guilty." This was the first time we had heard the voice of Donald Edward Reese.

The judge then asked defense and prosecution if they had anything more to say and they did not. He went back to Reese again and asked if there was anything else he wanted to say.

He said, "I ought to have mercy . . . I've been a Christian all my life. And all the good I've done, I don't think it's fair to be charged with something I didn't do and be letting the rest of the people down by keeping me locked up where I can't do anything at all. I'd like for you to spare my life, your Honor."

"Anything else?"

"Your Honor, that is all."

"Very well. You may be seated. . . ."

The judge then sentenced him on Count 1, the murder of Mr. Watson: ". . . it's the judgment and sentence of this Court that you be remanded to the custody of the sheriff of Jefferson County, then and there to be transported to the Department of Corrections of the State of Missouri, in the city of Jefferson and County of Cole, and there to receive at the hand of the State of Missouri the ultimate penalty of death as that offense was imposed by a jury of your peers."

And on count 2: ". . . it is the judgment and sentence of this Court that you be remanded to the custody of the sheriff of Jefferson County, then and there to be transported to the Department of Corrections of the State of Missouri, then and there to serve a term of life without the possibility of parole for the death of Christopher Griffith."

The judge then asked Reese if he had any complaints to make about the attorneys who defended him.

After a long pause, he answered, "Yes."

The judge asked if he wanted the attorneys present and he said he did not. The attorneys, Kempton and Murphy, ever alert to the limitations of their client, asked to have time to consult with him before they left the courtroom; a recess was declared.

During the recess the judge removed his robe and came back to John and me and told us how much he had appreciated our letter. We thanked him for that and for the verdict which we knew took courage. His parting words were that he hoped some day our views on the death penalty "would prevail." As the judge made his way back to the front of the courtroom, it felt as if a door had opened just a crack and let some light into our sadness.

The court reconvened. Before the defense attorneys left the courtroom, the judge said to Reese, ". . . from the trial judge's point of view, you've had some of the best representation by attorneys that I have ever encountered in seventeen years as judge." He went on to say Kempton's presentation in the trial was "superb" and that Ms. Murphy in the death penalty phase ". . . gave one of the most profound arguments that I've ever heard before a jury." We could have said "amen" for indeed these two attorneys had given the defendant every chance he could have had; sometimes it was difficult to understand how they could defend someone so obviously guilty. But they were doing a job and they did it well. It seemed to be a case where only a legal snafu could have prevented Reese's being declared guilty.

After the attorneys left, the judge proceeded to question Reese as to why he thought he had not been well-represented. Reese said he thought some evidence was not "picked up", he said he had wanted to testify, he said he had wanted input into the jury selection, and so on. After perhaps fifteen minutes of patient interrogation, the judge did not find probable cause for ineffective assistance although new attorneys were to be obtained for the appeal which had already been filed.

After the judge retired, both defense attorneys, Mark Kempton and Linda Murphy, came to us, shook our hands and thanked us for sharing our views with the judge. We in turn complimented them for their handling of a very difficult case with intelligence and compassion. Conspicuously absent from our fan club were the attorneys for the prosecution.

We left the courtroom with a lightness in our hearts we had not felt since Chris's death. We felt the action of the judge was a tribute to Chris and the way he had tried to live. Throughout the trial the judge had conducted himself in a thoughtful and caring manner. We felt uplifted by the sentence and by his attention to our feelings. Furthermore, we were impressed by him as a judge. He had treated both sets of attorneys with courtesy. And Reese, a man whose educational level was a GED and whose answers were halting and sometimes incomprehensible, was accorded thoughtful patience and respect. With a judge like that in the system (and we hope there are others), we the people may have more power than we think.

We have articles from four different newspapers on the sentencing, all of them quite accurate and focused on the cutting of the sentence in Chris's case. Headlines of these articles read:

QUAKERS WIN LIFE FOR KILLER

—*St. Louis Post-Dispatch*, May 6, 1988

JUDGE ACCEDES TO PLEAS, CUTS ONE DEATH SENTENCE

— *Kansas City Times*, May 6, 1988

SENTENCE SOLACE TO GRIFFITHS

— *Columbia Daily Tribune*, May 6, 1988

JUDGE LISTENS TO FAMILIES OF MURDER VICTIMS

— *The Missourian*, May 6, 1988

The last of these headlines was not really accurate. John and I were the only members of our family who participated in asking for the life sentence, and we were only a piece of one family. We chose not to involve our other three sons in our actions, realizing it is hard enough to present the views of two persons as one. Each of our sons is entitled to his own view and the expression of that view. They were supportive of our right to articulate and act upon our own feelings, realizing the importance of this expression to our healing.

We have been asked how we felt about media coverage. Sometimes it was gory and made us shudder with horror, but we've no reason to think it was inaccurate. The reporters were doing a job. The reporter from the *Columbia Daily Tribune*, Tom O'Sullivan, was especially considerate; he knew our views on the death penalty but did not divulge them until we felt comfortable about it.

Again, doing her job, Kim Bell of the *St. Louis Post-Dispatch*, wrote a feature article June 15, 1987 on the case headlined SUSPECT'S SUPPORTERS QUESTION HIS CONFESSION IN FOUR KILLINGS. In it, she presented Donald Reese from the viewpoint of family and friends. "... With a pack of colored pencils and a crisp sheet of white paper, Reese sketches Jesus, his savior. The Lord's hands are open and his arms point to the sky. ... When he's not drawing, Reese, 44, reads the Bible."

At the time we saw the article, less than a year after Chris's death, we were upset at such a presentation of Reese. After all, this man had killed our son. In looking back at the article, I feel less critical than I did then. On the one hand, in those months between his arrest and the trial, he might have been trying to build an image although I doubt he is that canny. Even so, he is entitled to do whatever he can to live with what he has done to the victims, their families, his family, and friends of us all. I found the portrayal of him as a religious person difficult to understand. I can give him that now; then I thought he should suffer.

A young woman writer who became a friend of ours, Karen Uhlenhuth of the *Kansas City Times* (now merged with the *Kansas City Star*), asked if she could write a feature article on the unlikely connection between Chris's death and the nonviolent beliefs of Chris and his parents. The article came out April 2, 1988, after the trial and before the sentencing, and included excerpts from interviews with Christopher's co-workers and friends, as well as from us. Karen had attended several days of the trial in preparation for writing the article.

People said, and probably hoped, the trial would help us "put it all behind us." In a letter to our family on May 10, 1988, a week after the sentencing, I wrote, "... Often we wonder why? Why did this happen? But then, we look around us, and we see that we are not the only people beset by tragedy. It is all around. We have concluded for now that there doesn't seem to be a reason why some suffer this kind of pain and others don't. It just is, and we have to live through it and go on. Part of living through it for us has been sharing with you all. Thank you for letting us bring you into our pain."

No, the trial and sentencing did not put it behind us; it will continue to be with us. The trial was just one more step on our journey through life without Chris. Most of the time now we are more philosophical about this tragedy than we once were. We are, through this experience, more aware than ever that life takes turns and one follows the turns as they appear. The road we were on before Chris's death is behind us; Chris's death is a part of all the time we have ahead of us. We cannot forget Chris; we cannot forget how he died. We can only integrate his death into our lives and go on down the path.

Chapter Sixteen

IN MEMORIAM, CHRISTOPHER

If I had the throat of a turtle dove;
I'd mourn, I'd mourn,
If I had the wings of an eagle,
I'd fly, I'd fly;
Fly to the heavens and call on God
To bring some comfort here.

If I had a heart so clear,
I'd laugh, I'd laugh,
And if I knew the future,
I'd cry, I'd cry,
But I have only love and grief for you,
Grief that time will turn to love again.

If I could wield love like a sword
I'd rage against death,
And if I had the touch of an angel
I'd heal your wounds,
But I have only hands
That can't reach you,
Hands that can only hold the living.

All that we can do for you

Is to go on living,
All that we can give you
Is to give your love to others;
The best things in your life,
Your dreams, your courage,
Live on to guide us in our exile here.
Song by Sylvia Thomas
Sung at Standing Reunion, Summer 1988

The 1988 Standing reunion was in June, again at Bear Creek Meetinghouse near Earlham, Iowa.

While we were eager to go, thoughts of the 1985 reunion brought back poignant memories: memories of Chris caring for my mother (both of them now dead) with a good-natured tenderness; of Chris singing in the talent show and competing in the George and Deborah Look Alike contest; of Chris, the adult, visiting family with an interest comparable to folks of our generation. With the remembrances came the recurring pain at his absence in our lives.

I put together a small folder about his life and death for people at the reunion, knowing some of them had not heard of his death and others would be interested in knowing more about it, especially those who had become acquainted with him three years before. In the introduction I wrote: "Three years ago Chris was at the Standing Reunion with us. He had a wonderful time here among all of you, his relatives, many of whom he met for the first time. He visited, sang and learned about the Standings. He had reached a place in his life where his roots were important to him. One of the most tender memories of the reunion in 1985 was his care of his grandma, Lydia Standing Thompson. To Wanda and me he said, 'You just go on and have a good time. I'll take care of Grandma.' And he did.

"John and I felt such pleasure in the way Chris related to you all. His joy in being here touched us in a deep and tender spot. We are glad we have that time, and many others . . . to remember."

Being at this reunion of extended family was good for us. They treated us with tenderness and praised Chris; at the same time, they encouraged us to live in "the now" while remembering Chris. The meetinghouse was familiar and comforting. It was here I first attended meeting as an infant in a basket; it was here I often sat in meeting as a child and youth — sometimes impatient, sometimes drinking in a special kind of peace — and it was here Christopher's father and I vowed before some of these very relatives forty-one years before to be together "as long as we both shall live." Even the view out the window at the front — tops of trees swaying in the breeze — was soothing. And the musty old smell of the meetinghouse was like salve on a wound.

On the first day of the reunion, we honored those who had died since the reunion in 1985. In memory of Chris, my sister played the tape made at the previous reunion of Chris singing his own composition *Indigo Bunting Day* in the talent show. It seemed as if he were foretelling his own death in the next to the last verse as he sang, "When I die, oh I die, My soul will always fly, With that lovely indigo bird, While the meadowlark's song is heard."

As his voice filled the meetinghouse, it brought back the memory of Chris three years before, his tall body folded into a chair between the facing benches, wearing his blue-and-white checked shirt, auburn head bent over his guitar, intent upon his music. He was trying to be casual but it was obvious to me that he took singing before this family group very seriously. As he finished the song, he made a little run on the guitar and looked out at his audience with a wide smile. It was as if he were asking to be liked. And he was liked. Very much.

Another special moment at the 1988 reunion was when Sylvia Thomas, a cousin a few years younger than Chris, sang, in her clear soprano voice, a song she had written in memory of Chris and another friend who had been murdered. The song is printed at the first of this chapter.

On July 25, 1988 John and I celebrated Christopher's fortieth birthday. As we had felt our way along grief's path, we decided to deal with difficult anniversary days (birthdays and death days) by doing something Chris would have enjoyed doing with us. So we went to Independence and toured the home of Harry and Bess Truman, looking at it as if Chris were with us. As we viewed with surprise the old-fashioned red and green kitchen with its 1950's stove and the overall simplicity of the house, John, remembering Chris's own tastes, said, "Chris would have appreciated the way they lived." We had a soda at a restaurant across the street from where the bus tour ended. Then we returned home and ate our dinner out, again at Chris's favorite Chinese restaurant.

Anniversaries are difficult; you mark the time between birth and death, and it seems too short. In thinking of Chris, we remembered the giddy joy of the birth of our first-born and the cutting sadness at his death. Two birthdays now had passed since Christopher's death. We had not seen him since before his thirty-eighth birthday. How I still regret we had not made a trip to Columbia as we had promised we would! Now we can never fulfill that promise.

The other anniversary — the date of his death — came September 9. John and I left Kansas City shortly before noon for the Swan Lake Wildlife Refuge near Sumner, Missouri. A giant fiberglass goose, several men high, is perched in a grassy spot in the middle of a small park at the edge of Sumner. The goose was built by a friend of our son Tim; we recalled Tim's telling us of the laborious process of getting the goose from Kansas City, where it was created, to Sumner. We admired the goose from all angles and then drove around the refuge for a while, not seeing much wildlife but feeling in touch with the kind of environment that Chris loved. On the way home we listened to the tape of his songs; in some ways it was harder then to listen to his voice than it had been in the first weeks after his death. Death, more final as time passes, felt more real.

We went to bed that night, our hearts sad at the loss we (and the rest of the world) had suffered. The third year of life without Chris had begun.

In subsequent years, we have continued to find ways to "be with" Chris on the anniversaries of his birth and death. On his most recent birthday, his forty-fourth, we went to the Arabia Museum on the Kansas City riverfront of the Missouri River where thousands of artifacts from a sunken riverboat, the *Arabia*, reside. We laughed when we imagined Chris, in his eager excitement, plying the guides with off-the-wall questions. Often on these anniversary days, we still listen to the tape of Chris singing his songs.

There was a third annual Christopher Griffith Memorial Run/Walk/Bike Event May 7, 1989. It differed from the first two in that there was no competition, no fundraising for the Children's Miracle Telethon, and fewer people. It was a time of coming together and exercising our bodies in honor of Chris who believed in doing just that. There were serious moments as we talked of Chris although we concentrated on enjoying the time together. Thirty-five or so people participated. Several young children did the course in strollers; a father and son rode bicycles. An 82-year-old friend of Chris, John and me, Zoe Baur, started the walk only to have to retire to the parking lot for her nitroglycerine and a rest. Unlike the other two years, the atmosphere was not celebratory, although there was a quiet caring for one another and the memory of Chris.

We had spent the night before the walk with Suzy Morse, Chris's good friend (and ours). We told her how, several months before, we had stopped in Columbia, hoping to find the spot along Gans Creek where Chris had taken us the last time we visited him there. John was sure he could go to it; I felt reasonably certain I could go to it; surely, together we could find it. Well, we wandered up hills and through valleys, and could not find it. Finally we asked Claire (a friend of Christopher's who lived in the house where he used to live). She gave us directions which we followed with care, we thought, parking at the end of a road as directed. Then we started toward the creek. A fresh breeze cooled us on that warm and sunny October day. We followed the path through open prairie and wooded areas, scrunching through the crispy leaves which carpeted the ground.

After about a mile of pleasant walking, we reached the bluff above the creek. Alas, we did not find the spot we remembered, though we located a place Chris would have liked on the bluff, and we sat there thinking of him.

Suzy assured us she could find the spot and offered to take us there. So after the walk we stopped at a deli where we bought sandwiches and drink for a picnic and set out once more in search of Chris's special place. We found it, and there on a large rock surface many feet above the quiet little creek, we had a picnic in the sun and reminisced about Chris. He would have liked our picnic.

Later, at home, we wrote to Carmen Abbott, Chris's former supervisor at Rusk who had been responsible for the three Run/Walk/Bike events, telling her not to feel an obligation to continue the event any longer than purposeful for those friends and colleagues who still remained in Columbia. It had been a balm to us for three years. It would be a priority for us if it were held again, but a number of Chris's friends had left Columbia and time had passed. (There was no Fourth Annual Christopher Griffith Run/Walk/Bike Event.)

In the third year after Chris's death, we attended meetings of The Compassionate Friends less frequently. While it is sometimes hard to recall how one felt at a given time in life, I don't believe I'll ever forget how wounded I felt for months after Chris's death. I remember thinking of Mitzi, the family dog when I was young. Mitzi had an incurable obsession for chasing Daddy's orange Allis Chalmers tractor. She was often injured in this pursuit although injury didn't stop her once her wounds had healed. When she was injured, she would make a cool nest in the dark, moist dirt up next to the house and lie there whimpering. I often felt like Mitzi in those early months.

It was because of our own painful memories of the months after Chris's death that we continued to attend The Compassionate Friends from time to time. The unconditional acceptance of our suffering in those early months helped hold us up. We could talk of Chris and his death and cry or not cry or be angry or whatever we needed to be and there was no judgment, no attempt to rationalize why this happened to us or to dispense any magic prescription to make us better. Just acceptance.

The pitfall in being part of this wonderful group is the possibility of hanging onto the early stages of grief longer than necessary as new people with fresh grief enter into the fellowship. We see this as something to watch for in ourselves. It is evident that grief is individual, that while the theory of "stages" seems sound, people differ in sequence and time of grief. In the third year, we began to see our function in The Compassionate Friends group to help rather than be helped. In the last two years, we have seldom attended, although we hope to continue to be involved with the organization at some level in gratitude for what the group did for us. For some parents, especially at first, it is a bridge between totally succumbing to grief and beginning to work through the horrible reality of loss of a child.

Through a friend from The Compassionate Friends, I had the opportunity to speak several times, along with others who have experienced grief through death of family members, to third- and fourth-year medical students at the University of Missouri-Kansas City. Mary Spratt, who herself lost a son named Christopher to a rare disease some years ago, teaches a class where there is a one-day session on grief and the relationship of the medical profession to the grieving. As a resource person, I discussed my own grief experience, answered questions from the students, made personal observations about the grief process. Although I was uncomfortable speaking in public, and speaking of Chris is sometimes difficult, I felt good about letting bright young future physicians know how it feels, what helps and what doesn't help.

John also had opportunities to educate; several times he spoke on the death penalty to classes at St. Teresa's Academy. The young man who taught the class felt a view from the perspective of the victim's family would be valuable for his students.

Both of us have been involved in the Western Missouri Coalition Against the Death Penalty. Through contact with this group we attended, in the third year, a vigil where John spoke against the death penalty from the view of the parent of a murdered son.

During the 1990 session of the Missouri legislature, we were told we would be asked to testify before the Missouri House Committee on Civil and Criminal Justice regarding House Bill 1486, but by some oversight, we were not notified of the hearing. This bill provided for a five-year moratorium of the death penalty in Missouri; a commission would have been appointed to study the issues surrounding the death penalty during a five-year interim when no person would be put to death by the state. Although we would rather see abolition of the death penalty, we supported the bill as a step in the right direction. We were disappointed not to be called to testify. (The bill did not pass.)

John, who does a good job of being prepared, had already written a four-page statement for the committee. A small portion of the statement follows: "... When this sort of thing happens it is inevitable, I think, that a parent wants to scream to the very heavens: Why? How could this horrible injustice happen in what our religious leaders have assured us is a moral universe? Certainly that is one of the reactions my wife and I had. We literally felt like screaming — Why? ...

"The contemporary secular answer to this question seems to be that Donald Reese murdered our son, and Donald Reese must pay like price for that murder. Christopher's murder is an unfortunate aspect of existence in our society, but if the state kills Donald Reese we, as a society, have done all we can to even the score. This answer doesn't satisfy me any more than the religious belief that God has, through this murder, called Chris to heaven. . . .

"In struggling with these questions a conviction has taken hold in my mind and has only strengthened with the passage of time. That conviction is that our collective human consciousness, as expressed in our society's values, must also bear responsibility for the murder of our son. In a profound sense, we all share in that responsibility. . . ."

At this time, the legislative plan of the Western Missouri Coalition Against the Death Penalty is to chip away at the death penalty with specific exclusions. In 1991 the coalition drafted an unsuccessful bill which excluded the mentally retarded from the death penalty. In 1992 efforts to exclude the mentally retarded from the death penalty were thwarted when that legislation got buried in the "concealed weapons" bill which fortunately was not passed. The coalition also plans to direct renewed energy in education toward the abolition of the death penalty. John is still active in the coalition and I support it although I cannot usually attend meetings because of a conflict in my schedule.

During the years since Chris's death, the activities of our lives have gone on — involvement in the Iowa Yearly Meeting of Friends (Conservative) and Scattergood Friends School, Missouri Valley Conference of Friends and our own meeting; work with the American Friends Service Committee; reading, writing, exercising. All of these activities keep our minds and bodies active, and active minds are less likely to get on the merry-go-round of self-pity. Besides we truly believe Chris would not want us to mope; he would want us to "be happy, don't worry," not easy when his dear absent face keeps flashing through our minds.

Our three other sons and their wives have given us the support of love and caring, all in different ways. The now five grandchildren, in their priceless innocence, have directed our attention to the world of the future. We have found that with Chris's death, the dynamic of our family has undergone change. With his death, something was missing. Like a machine, the Griffith family, as all families, had been built unconsciously, piece by piece. For years it purred along (knocking and sputtering at times) with Chris performing his function as eldest son. Now that he was gone, we looked (and still look) for ways to go on without him.

Each of us has initiated changes, sometimes dramatic, sometimes subtle, as we have coped with this space that looms in our family. For each of us, there are profound questions as we ponder life and death, relationships with one another and others, and how we are to live in this world of unexpected, sometimes awful, change. I believe we have made honest efforts to try not to answer or even to articulate one another's questions, to try to accept one another as we search for answers in our own ways.

In preparation for writing this book, I asked Tim, Jon and Ben for any contributions they might care to make. Tim and Ben responded during the first two years to this difficult request; their responses are within these pages. Jon did not feel able to respond until this letter August 7, 1990:

> Dear Mom:
>
> Well, I've spent the last few nights trying to write something about Chris's murder, and I honestly can't. I think you'd better go on without me. I think it's just all too close for me to do a very good job of it. I

either start feeling depressed or what I end up writing sounds so trite and not at all what I felt. If you want, here are some of the ideas I had which you could use or not use, whatever you think best.

I wanted to write some paragraphs about the last time Chris came to visit us down here. It was really the best time we'd had with a visitor for quite awhile. We went to Nancy's parents' house and stayed there for a weekend (her parents were away). One of the nicest times was when the four of us went floating down the Blanco River on air mattresses, just talking and letting the current take us while Thea swam from person to person and got out of the river and hunted up on the bank. It was really pleasant, and Chris could be quite funny and we just had a good talk.

I wanted to write about the same visit when one noon Chris decided he wanted to fix us some string beans, so in the rain, he went out to the garden and picked what beans were left on our vines. I remember watching him from the dining room window as he stood up in a gray poncho and proceeded to eat a long bean right there in the garden. I'm not sure why, but the image struck me as quintessential Chris and I called Nancy to the window so we could both watch, something he didn't know we were doing.

The first year was horrendous, and like everyone else I think Jeri, Nancy and I were changed completely and utterly by the whole experience. There was a point where I knew I had to stop the suffering and grief if I could. I was out of work, and I was interviewing for jobs, and I suspect that employers thought I looked odd, because I was odd. I felt completely outside the whole system of having and making a life, and I knew it was guilt about him dying and me going on, but I couldn't stop myself. I worked a job at University of Texas for six months before I even told anyone there that my brother had been murdered, and then I had to say something since I was asking for funeral leave (for the burial of Chris's ashes in June). If Jeri and Nancy told someone about it at our house, I'd just leave the room, not to get sympathy, but because I just couldn't stand to hear about it. Those times are past, but I'd have to say it was only recently that I could talk to anyone about it.

I wanted to say something too about recognizing what a difficult experience it was for so many people. I think about Chris's friends in Columbia who heard about it that first day and had to wait out the information. I think about the one friend who identified the body. I think about Tim who had to call you two at Grandma's and then probably didn't sleep the rest of the night. I think about you and Dad driving home in the dark, and how lonely and awful you must have felt. Whenever I remember how I felt those first few days, I think about those things, and I truly believe you all had the more difficult tasks. I don't see how you did it. Anyway, Mom, feel free to use anything you want and feel free to write whatever you want in your own words. I'm sorry I'm not much of a help. I hope you get a draft soon that you feel good about. .

Much love, Jon

Chris's former roommate, John Markovitz, and Kim Brown were married September 21, 1990. We were invited to the wedding, but since we were to have weekend guests, we were unable to attend. As I shopped for a gift to send to John and Kim, the idea of imagining Chris helping me buy a gift he would have liked for them to have took hold of me. "We" bought a bread plate and knife which I sent along with a letter of regret. John wrote later, "... I read the letter at the reception (I hope you don't mind) and spoke of Chris at the ceremony. Many people thanked me for acknowledging him." As proof that life goes on, we received announcement some months later of the birth of Louis "Blue" Christopher Markovitz. It touched us to know that love and caring for Chris goes on in such a special way.

Some friends ask us how we are feeling now. And we usually say we are getting along fine, or all right, or so-so, or ... whatever. Having people ask shows that others still recognize the reality of Chris.

The sharpness of the pain has lessened, but it is still there. It surfaces at unexpected times and places. There is not a day but what I think of Chris for some reason or other; sometimes my eyes sting with tears, and sometimes (less often as time goes on) the hopelessness of anger sweeps through me. Sometimes I remember something amusing and I laugh; sometimes it is only an awareness of Chris and who he was that seeps through the ordinariness of my day.

He is not forgotten. The grief at his death goes on in a more quiet, sedate way; it is not raw as it once was. This year the sixth anniversary of his death passed; we acknowledge we are indeed able to live without his physical presence. However, I believe there is a special spot in our hearts where pain at his death and joy at having had him for a son will mingle into eternity. Yes, we are living through the experience and will continue to do so, probably forever.

Chapter Seventeen

REMEMBERING CHRIS
1991

Five years
And still I wonder
Where you are.

Fanciful,
I think you may ride
On a cloud.

The day breath
Left you
White billowy clouds
Floated in the sky.

Did the "you" leave
Your dying body and
Leap skyward?

Or did a low flying hawk
Catch the "you"?
If so, your friend saw you
Circle her house
Only days after . . .

Or when I think of you,
Call your name,
Do you come
And walk beside me,
An invisible hand on my shoulder?

But I must stop this —
I know you live on
In us,
I know that,
I feel it every day.
That's surely
Enough.

Still, I want
There to be more.

— Reva Griffith, 1991

When I began the story of Chris I didn't really know where I was going. I only knew I needed to write it. In the early weeks, I fumbled around trying to get a direction. Finally, I just wrote, asking for input from family and friends. What has emerged, I believe, is a personal story of grief and a memorial to Chris.

I have intended to tell the story of the life and death of Christopher Griffith with enough clarity that it stands without a conclusion. For there really is no conclusion — it goes on. Yet, at this point, I want to pause between movements of one of life's symphonies for further reflection.

In many ways, Chris lived an ordinary life; yet the ways in which he lived and related to his world were extraordinary because they were his ways. In that sense, I suppose all of us are extraordinary.

So how was Chris extraordinary? What set him apart from others? What gave his life special meaning? How can it be defined?

Most of us hope we will leave advocates here on earth when we die — friends and family who will praise and defend the lives we led. We may hope they will at times exaggerate our virtues. Perhaps, in the afterglow of our lives, they will overlook some of our faults. As we go about the dailiness of living, we may (probably in secret) hope that something positive will make our lives stand out, that we will not have lived without making some noticeable contribution to those with whom we live and move and have our being for the unpredictable span of days we are allowed on this earth.

In the darkness of the night after we learned of Chris's death, we drove from northwest Iowa toward Kansas City. In the silence of that journey, with burdened hearts and voices strange with pain, we, his parents and staunchest advocates, reflected on his life.

One of us said, "He really tried to do the right thing."

The other, "He was a gentle man."

We agreed, "He was our friend," sensing that this realization in itself might be extraordinary.

And so it went through the night.

And in the light of the morning, as our world and Christopher's world learned of his death, we discovered we were not alone; Chris had a host of advocates. The numbers and identities of the people who spoke and wrote of the specialness of this man amazed us and warmed our sore hearts. They were important to our consolation.

A few of them speak below:

Isabel Griffith, 'Grandmommie,' says, "Chris Griffith was pure sunshine. When he entered a room, everyone's spirits were uplifted. His upbeat nature must have helped his physical therapy child-patients make some almost miraculous improvement. My sisters and I would sit enthralled as, at our request, Chris told about experiences with 'his' children."

"... At that moment the world with Chris in it seemed so right and so hopeful and my spirit was buoyed up just by being with him. I hope," writes Nancy Osborn, "to remember that feeling always — this is what Chris has left as his gift to me."

His Aunt Wanda writes, "We *loved* knowing him, and we feel his thoughts and presence so often. Sometimes I think of how we wonder so much about death, and we know, as in birth, we all have to experience it alone. And now Chris, so much younger than I, knows this mystery.

"I had a vision after his death that was so real, and still is, that I can hardly be convinced it didn't happen. I heard a car drive in — it was a gold Datsun pickup; I went to the back door and Chris got out and yelled, 'Hi, Aunt Wanda!' And then the whole picture dissolved, but his message lingers on. I believe he lives!"

From his cousin, Mary Griffith Fuller, come these words, "... One of the key teachings of Buddhism is that 'Death comes without warning' so it is necessary to practice very hard in this lifetime because you never know when it might end. I had never experienced the reality of that before Chris died."

Steve Call, one of Chris's former roommates, married Teresa Sweeney, another friend, some months after Chris's death. In response to a request for permission to include her poem about Chris in the book, Teresa wrote, "... I hope that this book will give what Chris gave to so many, his great smile and his love. Steven wants *Elegy* to speak for both of us and, really, I hope it speaks for more than both of us. ..."

ELEGY

In Memory of Christopher Griffith

Chris, the world has changed, each day another
without you, song and incantation fade.

It's like watching our hands unfold,
watching as we let go of the rope thrown

out to you and seeing you struggle as the boat grows
distant, as the life you once called yours

has grown. And now it's gone. We tried pulling
you back but kept knocking against the hard

surface of fact where memory loses hold
and the future looms ahead like tracks

leading to a bridge . . . but the bridge is down.
And you want to say stop, say

stop to the train, but you go on hurtling
forward, we go on, without you, to a place

we once called hope, and now simply call our lives.
After you died, Steven and I tried

to return ourselves to the world
grown dark without you, tried to make

the world stay. A voiceless incantation
which slowly, now two autumns past, has given

root to voice. The medicine feeds what it's meant
to allay. Lost in the crossing over, left

with you and without you, we see the shadowy
adding up and accounting that life brings.

Its abrupt falling away . . . Until we understand
this distance that begins inside and travels

to a place we have not yet arrived, the long path
of our death. Until we arrive, here in our unordered

violent world, we take you in, attempt creation
of another end, one suffused with the possibility

of the life you led, the life left hanging, the life
you believed was song, remedy against the world.
— Teresa Sweeney, 1988

Francis Baumli, a close friend, sent some unique personal reflections on what Chris's death has meant to him. We have found these comments very meaningful; I quote from them here.

". . . I refer to the man who murdered Chris. I have often thought of him, and have been struck by the circumstances preceding his murder of Chris. Realizing those circumstances causes me to be more acutely aware of how we all are responsible for the violence that happens in this world. One does not have to be an existentialist to assume this stance, and I do not here assume it as a way of expiating the anger I feel toward Chris's murderer. . . ."

He goes on to recount the circumstances of Reese's life: underemployment, bills, his wife having left him and taken the children, broke, etc. He also suggests the probable emotions which resulted — anger, fear, loneliness, frustration.

". . . All those things caused him to kill; yet, what might have caused him to act otherwise? I have thought to myself: What if, that morning when he had driven to the quarry, hoping to be given work, the person hiring had said, 'I'm sorry, we don't have anything for you today, but you're a good worker; I'll do my best to make sure you have something tomorrow.'

"Or, suppose that morning, his estranged wife had come by and said, 'I'm sorry things didn't work out between us. It's probably not any more your fault than mine. But these are still your kids. You're their father. Why don't you take them for the day . . . I've packed their lunches. Enjoy them, and I'll come by this evening to pick them up.' Or, maybe all that would have been necessary, to keep this fellow from snapping — from crossing over that line to violence — would have been something no more complicated than being smiled at, in a genuine and friendly way, by a stranger as he was walking from his house to his vehicle.

"All these things I have thought, and often it has crossed my mind when I look upon someone who appears to be depressed, or angry, that here is a person in need, maybe in the same kind of need as was that man who murdered Chris, and this person is weak, like all of us, and could do violence, as could all of us; but here, if I but show one gesture of good will, maybe I will have helped this person, and, maybe I will have, without ever knowing, be that small bit of good cheer which gives another human being enough respite from their anguish that they do not cross over that line into terrible violence. Thus, from Chris's death, my life has taken on new meaning. . . ."

Does not this give one pause? What if these words were taken seriously in our world? Would not Chris's life and death have meaning? Would not practice of the way of life Chris tried to live make a difference? We believe so.

Other Ways His Life Continues . . .

We have spoken before of Chris's interest in men's issues and of the founding of BRAVO (Brothers Resolved Against Violence and Oppression) and MMRG (Mid-Missouri Men's Resource Group). I like to think of the men who have over the years found help, maybe even life-changing help, as suggested by Francis above, in BRAVO.

Ben, our youngest son, and Ron Knight, my nephew the same age as Chris, both of whom lived in Kentucky at the time of Chris's death, were inspired by Chris's involvement in men's issues. In memory of Chris and out of their own need to talk, they helped start a men's discussion group among their friends in central Kentucky. Called ARGO and begun in 1987, the group met, often monthly, for two years "to support, express and explore ideas, to feel and to care."

In a September 1988 newsletter of the group, Ben wrote, "ARGO has enabled me to deal much better with the murder of my brother Chris. ARGO has led me to a healthier and deeper relationship with my wife; ARGO has given me a better understanding of gender issues, and finally it has given me some friends with whom I can share anything. . . ."

Although ARGO has not met recently (distance is a problem), its two-year existence may well have helped its members learn to speak with one another and with other men about men's issues in a real and meaningful way. We believe it served a useful purpose.

A physical therapy scholarship in Chris's name has been established at the University of Missouri-Columbia. Interest from a sum of money set aside from his estate by Tim, Jon, Ben, John and me is to be used each year to aid physical therapy students who have financial need and who have demonstrated a caring attitude toward patients and other students. Perhaps Chris's legacy of concern for others will carry on in a small way in his chosen profession. Several physical therapy students who have received Christopher Griffith scholarship awards have written to us, tangible reminders that the caring attitude attributed to Chris by his co-workers is encouraged and carried on.

We Are Often Reminded of Chris . . .

When Tim called us at my parents' home in northwest Iowa and said, ". . . and he killed Chris and the others," we were jerked without warning onto a new path on our life's journey. Instead of going "that way" with a Chris in our lives, we are going "the other way" without his smiling, caring presence. Along this other way, there are remembrances of him.

We are reminded of Chris when we travel in eastern Missouri. A trip we took in October of 1989, over three years after Chris's death, is a poignant example. John and I came back through the Ozarks from a visit with Ben and family in Kentucky. As we drove up a portion of highway 21 designated on the map as "scenic," we realized we would go by Potosi, the town where Donald Reese, in a state prison, awaits his fate on death row. The day, up until then bright with autumn, faded, as the familiar wash of sorrow moved through us.

Then, further down the road, as we approached Columbia, regrets for the visits we might have had with Chris in Columbia, welled up. We like Columbia because Chris loved being there, and because many of his friends, our friends, are still there. On the other hand, when the memories of time spent there with him come rushing back, we can't help thinking of how we used to stop in Columbia to say hello to Chris and experience the warmth of his being; now he's not there.

That day in Columbia we drove to Rusk Rehabilitation Center to see the painting and plaque dedicated in Chris's memory over three years before. The visit was a lesson in change. We didn't remember exactly where the painting was so we asked a young woman at a reception desk on first floor to direct us to it. She didn't know what we were talking about.

We looked at each other with a "so that's how it is so soon" expression and proceeded to second floor, following our own instincts, where we found the painting and plaque in a glass case on the wall outside the area where physical therapy patients were being treated. Except for a curious glance or two in our direction, we were ignored. We wondered how many of the patients and staff ever looked in that case at the painting and picture of the young man who, only a few short years before, in his own unique and caring manner, treated patients in that very room. We took a picture of the case and returned to our car, painfully aware of how quickly the world adjusts to the absence of those who die. As new sprigs of green replace those which wither and die, so do we absorb spaces once filled by the fallen among us.

On down the road toward Kansas City is the Marshall exit from highway 70, near the firing range where Chris spent his last minutes, minutes we still think of with pain. We wonder what went through his mind as he died there. Sometimes I think of the entry below which I found in a journal he kept the summer of 1984.

> *August 13, 1984:* "Well, I feel that some significant things are happening in my life. One is the recognition that I really believe that there is a power and force that is in this world. I felt it on my trip to the Northwest and I have felt it a number of times since my return to Columbia. It is a dynamic yet subtle force. I have felt this power. . . ."

Did he feel this "power" in his dying moments? Oh, how I hope he did!

There are pictures and mementoes of Chris in our house. A collage of Chris (along with pictures of his brothers and their families) is on our mantel. Two quilted wall hangings crafted in memory of Chris grace our walls. One, called *The Colors of Chris*, was done by Rachel Knight, my nephew Ron's former wife; it is an intricate design of strips of fabric, on one of which there are five happy dancing bears, reminiscent of Chris himself. The other hanging, *Indigo Bunting Day*, named for Chris's song of that title, was pieced by his cousin, Joyce Osborn; a circle of eight lively indigo buntings in flight is the focal point of this work.

There are two mounted four-leaf clovers on the bookcase. One is in a little white frame. It took its place the first Christmas after Chris's death, accompanied by this message from Ben, "This clover was in one of Chris's songbooks, and it is to remind us of how lucky we were to have Chris, and of the good things that are still moving because of his life." (Some people, including my mother and Chris, seem to have a special knack for finding four-leaf clovers.) The other clover was sent to us in 1988 by Tom, my sister's youngest child. In the letter that came with the clover he said he had found it in the meetinghouse yard at Bear Creek some years ago and wanted us to have it in memory of Chris.

Two crystals hang in south windows of our house. One of these is a "Chris Crystal" sent to us by my sister a month or so after Christopher's death to remind us of Chris and his continuing light in the world. On sunny days, particularly cold winter days when the sun rides low in the southern sky, splashes of rainbow colors flash around our living and dining rooms. In this happy way we are reminded of Chris and what his existence brought to us and others. Our granddaughter, Jordan Bailey Griffith, born September 7, 1989, two days before the third anniversary of Chris's death, eagerly watches the rainbows, her head moving back and forth and up and down as the prisms dance on the walls. Someday we will tell her about the uncle she never knew and the crystal that flashes colors about in his memory.

An African violet — an unusual magenta color — found in Chris's house, blooms in the north window of our kitchen. Two of its offspring are being nurtured to maturity. A Dracaena, a birthday gift from Chris and Penny in 1986, is a living reminder of Chris as are a variety of other plants given us at the time of his death. Recently Penny told us Chris's good friend Andrew has a plant he gave Chris some years ago which he reclaimed at the time of Chris's death. Chris called it his "Andy" plant.

We live with some of Chris's possessions, now ours. I mix bread in a large aluminum mixing bowl which was Chris's; a small wooden table we (like Chris) plan to refinish is in our kitchen; a nifty heavy iron frying pan belonged to Chris; an old lamp in our living room was among his possessions; and so on. Both John and I wear items of his clothing; John, about Chris's size, wears his shirts, pants and shoes while I have two pairs of bib overalls I sometimes wear (they are too long but much loved) and a couple of oversized shirts. Maudlin? We don't think so. It gives us pleasure to know the fabric that touched his skin now touches ours.

In August 1990 we received word that we could pick up Chris's boots and watch, articles he was wearing at the time of his death, at the highway patrol office in Lee's Summit. For some reason we don't understand, these articles had been kept for evidence in the event they were needed in the appeals process. Although it was almost four years since his death, the watch was still running, off some minutes, even though the crystal was broken and there was a dent in the case that made it impossible to reset the watch. John took the watch to a digital watch repair shop some miles away. We could have bought a watch for less than it took to repair it, but it feels good to us to have it here as it continues to record the passing of time on this earth.

Chapter Eighteen

FRIEND, HEALER, BROTHER, SON
One day you were here . . .

A friend,
    Who listened with your heart.

A healer,
    With light and gentle ways.

A brother,
    Protector of secrets.

A son,
    Bearer of light.

Yes, one day you were here
And the next . . .
Gone.

Remembering your touch,
We must go on.
— Reva Griffith, March 1987

John Reflects on Chris's Death (4/18/90)...

For months following Chris's death it seemed that my mind was focused on Chris. Even when doing things necessary for daily existence, the thought of Chris continued. To try to channel this experience in a constructive way, I began to experiment with short phrases which I could mentally repeat. At first these phrases tended to be somewhat detailed. But finally I settled on a phrase of five words: "Chris — gentle friend, spiritual companion." Those five words reinforced in my mind what I perceived to be Chris's gift to me. The phrase was mentally repeated countless times over a period of many months.

I am now past this phase of the grief process. I still think of Chris most every day — perhaps every day — but I now am able to deal with the decisions of everyday life with more or less total concentration. At times I experience momentary surges of grief and of joy. Usually these experiences are related to reading something about Chris — his mother's poems, memories some friend shares in a letter or listening to a cassette recording of Chris singing his songs. At other times, the simple beauty of a stream, a flower or a bird in flight will make me think of Chris. Sometimes there are waves of grief which are completely unpredictable and cannot be associated with any particular experience. But these times are now less and less frequent.

In struggling with the problem of trying to make sense out of Chris's death, I find that I have come to a greatly strengthened sense of the universality of life. This sense of universality was especially strong the day we put Chris's ashes in the ground.

I did not record the words I spoke at that time, but the thought expressed was: "We hold the remains of Chris's body in this box. We tend to think of our bodies as being uniquely 'ours,' and it is easy to think of these ashes as being what is left of Chris's body. Yet there is not an atom in this box that was not in existence when the world began. Those atoms have been cycled and recycled countless times through the plants of the fields and the beasts of forests. They were recognized momentarily as Chris's *particular* body but are now returned to the earth to continue the celebration of the *universality* of life."

The interplay of the particular and the universal. I am fascinated by the vast genetic knowledge that is present in the first cell of a new human being. Enough knowledge we are told to fill a hundred encyclopedia volumes. Most of our responses to life are conditioned — either genetically or culturally — by a million, million experiences of other human beings. We are the product of our universality but we proudly cling to our particularity.

This feeling of the "continuum" quality of life has grown stronger with Chris's death. Who is responsible for Chris's murder? Of course we can point to the particular person known as Donald Reese. And inasmuch as we each play out our role of a particular human being endowed with some measure of freedom, we do have a measure of responsibility for our acts. But, to my mind, Donald Reese's murder of Chris is merely one sick expression of a sickness which we all share universally. At a deeper level than we care to acknowledge, we are all Donald Reese and we are all Chris Griffith. As this insight takes form, one becomes aware of the importance of each act of freedom. The world we live in is an expression of our universality.

How proud I am of the particular Chris Griffith who gave so much of his freedom to choose gentleness, love and compassion as his contribution to our universality. In my particular freedom, I know that it is profoundly important that I try to do likewise.

How It Is for Me Now . . .

John and I have each in our own way dealt with Chris's death as the days have passed. Sometimes we have faced it head-on; sometimes we have stepped aside to let the pain pass. Chris's death has influenced how we live and how we view life.

As time goes on I have learned to accept the fact of Chris's murder although it is still not acceptable to me that it happened, nor do I see it as having been ordained by some higher power. I feel this devastating event in our lives cannot be explained, any more than can similar events which have come to others. It happened and we must live with it.

As for resolution of my grief, for me so far I have experienced no magical moment when I have said, "I've resolved my grief." I don't expect or even want this moment. With grief, as with other experiences in life, I feel we continue to live with this life event and to put it into an evolving context in our lives. We can't change direction and move back to where we were before it happened; we must go forward with the knowledge and experience of the event. The happenings in our lives contribute to who we are as human beings. We can't throw them aside and say, "There, that is done." We can say, "This has happened to me. How will I deal with it?" Easy to say, hard to do; for as I look back on my grief for Chris, there have been times when "hanging on" is all I have been able to do.

In December 1991 John and I were privileged to stand at the bedside of a friend who was dying from complications of AIDS. He was aware that his death was imminent. At first he was caught up in arrangements for his dying and for distribution of the leavings of his life. Then a few days before his death, his attention shifted to dying. From then on, he wanted peace and quiet at his bedside; he seemed to be looking beyond where he lay. I took comfort in his gradual detachment from the things of this earth. At one point, I almost asked him to greet Chris for me, but the moment passed. I wish I had asked him.

Most of the time now I think I do what I need to do to carry on with my life and to relate as best I know how to others in this world. However, when I stop to examine my inner feelings, I know there is an undercurrent of sadness, even beyond missing Chris, that was not there before. Life and death are real; I am more conscious of the transitory nature of living. In life's scheme, I am aware how quickly we mortals become someone's memory. Chris, a man with everything to live for, was without warning taken away; he had no choice in the matter. Bad, incomprehensibly sad, things can and do happen to human beings we know and to us. I don't feel I carry this knowledge around as a burden; it's just that the recognition of the possibility of such happenings feels real and present as I experience the events of my particular life.

Thought of my own death, at my age seeming closer every day, has a different feel now. It's as if Chris has broken the way; if Chris can die, I can. With the fact of death established in the dramatic and unwelcome death of my oldest son, I, in my better moments, more actively aspire to make my finite time here worthwhile.

Sometimes I feel I am more compassionate because of the pain of Christopher's death. At first, sorrows of others, even those I read about in the paper, were heavy — mirrors of my own pain. Fortunately, I am now able to stand off at a more comfortable distance from the pain of others. Most of the time I can identify with and respond without being overwhelmed myself. Sometimes, much to my surprise, I process tragic events in the lives of others more casually than I did before Chris's death. It's as if there are times when I reach a point where my ability to compute more sorrow shuts down.

In my own experience, it is difficult — no, impossible — for me to separate unhappiness at everyday setbacks from below-the-surface sadness at Chris's death. For example, ever since a time of depression which began in the fall over thirty years ago, I have experienced some melancholia in late autumn. The fall I neared the end of the final draft of this book, I felt a more-than-usual melancholy. I wondered why. Was it because poring over these words kept me close to Chris? Did I fear cutting the strings that bound us in this effort? I believe it was yet another face of grief. And there will be more.

In a December 1990 meeting for worship at Penn Valley Meeting of Friends I said that the births of my children were some of the happiest moments of my life, and that the deaths of loved ones were some of the saddest.

I went on to tell of my first experience with the death of someone close to me. My grandfather died in 1936 when I was ten years old. In order to explain the disappearance of this dearly loved person in my life, I formulated my own belief in reincarnation. The explanation was that one of my aunts, who was pregnant at the time, was carrying the replacement for my grandpa. When the child was a boy, this belief was reinforced.

In meeting that day, I went on to say that as I grew older, read more about and attempted to analyze the meaning of death, the earlier simplistic way of dealing with death faded away. As more close family and friends died, I tried to accept a conventional belief in immortality — an attempt that was more hope than faith.

Here I want to expand upon on my concluding thoughts that day in meeting:

When Chris died, I had to face my own doubts. I really could not explain his death; I didn't know what happened to him. This desolation was reflected in the early poetry after his death. As the days and years have passed since his death, my feelings have gradually softened. I know of nothing to account for the change except for the passage of time and the inevitable and consuming struggle of integrating Chris's death into my being.

What happens at death still remains an unsolved mystery to me. However, I have become more accepting of the process of life which ultimately includes death. This does not mean that there will not be pain and tears at the deaths of those I love, for there will be.

Also, I have a lingering conviction that Chris's spirit lives. I can't explain this by logic. Apparently my Quaker upbringing of a belief in the presence of a spirit of love within each of us took. How can this spirit be destroyed?

As for Chris himself, I miss his being in our lives every day. When I am on my daily walks, I think about him. Holidays are not the same with him gone. We observe the anniversaries of his birth and death in a tangle of sorrow and joy. When someone asks me how many children I have, I am likely to reply, "Four sons," and sometimes I explain. It is clear I don't want to forget. Nor will I.

Some thoughts about grief. I cannot conclude this story without saying something to those who grieve for a son, daughter, or anyone. Since each of us is a unique combination of what is innate, genetic and experiential, we carry with us differing coping mechanisms. We will not grieve the same way or reach the same resolutions as we proceed with our lives after the death of someone we care for. It is important that we recognize this and find our own ways. John and I have not grieved in the same way nor with the same intensity at the same time as we have grieved for Chris, yet the realities of our separate griefs cannot be denied.

To those in fresh grief, I would say it is not likely you will hurt forever as you hurt now. The human mind and spirit can and do heal. Most of us could not endure if the intensity of early grief were to continue indefinitely. In the beginning the pain is great, but it does get less sharp. As it lessens, you may be concerned that you will forget the one for whom you grieve; this also is unlikely; the experience of her/his existence is part of you now and forever. Also, know that your life can go on after the death of the one you love although it will not feel the same as it did with that person in it with you. Try to find your own way to "live through" this thing and live the days ahead one at a time.

I read my own words and I smile, for I remember hearing similar words in those early weeks after Chris's death. And I said to myself, "That can't be true." But it has been. Waves of pain can engulf us and seem about to sweep us away. But the human spirit is not easily overcome. We can and do stand.

And to those who want to comfort the bereaved, I will share some thoughts from my own experience. As I have said above, reactions to the death of a loved one are not universal since our life experiences differ. For myself: I was not comforted with the idea that God wanted Chris with Him because he was one of the best; in the early days after his death, I didn't want to hear that Chris was in a better place than we are; I didn't need to be reminded that I had other wonderful family around me. *I did need to hear that Chris was loved, to feel that I was cared for.* At times I needed to let the tears flow if they would, to cry out if I felt like it.

Thinking back on my own experience, I believe it is usually best to begin with a simple "I'm sorry," to refrain from explanations as to why the death might have occurred, to be sensitive to what might bring comfort to the griever. Most bereaved persons cannot escape pain; it is unlikely you can explain it away. With the possible exception of long and/or debilitating illness, pain is usually part of separation by death.

Also, as time goes by, when a bereaved person talks about the loved one, realize this doesn't necessarily mean the person is hanging on to grief in an "unhealthy" way. Speaking of the person may help affirm the hope that that person will continue to live in the hearts and minds of those who knew her/him. Recognition of the existence of the one who died is important to those who suffer such a loss. And again, death as a part of the life process is not something to forget but something to remember as an intimate part of life.

In a diary of our experiences in the months soon after Chris's death, I wrote, "Both of us still see his face in our minds — and we are glad of it. His voice rings in our heads. We see his loping gait, his tall body, the mischievous gleam in

Photo by Andrew Sieff

Chris smiles for a friend in Columbia, MO.

his eye. We feel the embrace the three of us shared the last time we saw him. We treasure remembrances of him that surround us. Of course they make us sad, but they remind us of the existence of a precious person, our eldest son, who lives on within and around us."

Now, over six years later, this is still true.

> "... I really believe that there is a power and force that is in this world. ... I have felt this power ..."
>
> — Chris, 1984

EPILOGUE

When I began to write this epilogue, I thought it would be for our sons and their families. However, as I searched for the words, I realized I needed to write these things — for the family of course, but especially for me.

When a child in a family dies, no matter the age, thoughts and love seem to focus on the one who has died. As parents, we are so shattered by the death, so broken, that we may try to resurrect the missing one, to bring him/her back to us through remembering. After Chris's death, we concentrated on him — who he was, what he did, what he left. We remembered his many endearing qualities, few of the others. We recalled his hopes and dreams, and they stood up well. In our need to hold on, we were obsessed with Chris. We wanted others to know how much we loved him and all he had accomplished. The soreness of our hearts ached for healing, and his resurrection was part of that healing.

And Chris was a proper hero. I believe his brothers would agree. Not perfect — none of us is perfect — but heroic nonetheless. As we have grieved, we seem not to have looked at his imperfections although we have known they were there.

His brothers too, in their own ways, are fine and heroic. I see them as caring men who have tried (as Chris tried) to follow their own hearts. They have marched to the beat of the drummers they have heard, and the drum hasn't sounded the same to any of them. Like Chris, they too have had to adjust at times to modified beats as they, like all of us, have fumbled in the search for their own paths.

At the time of Chris's death, they were there for us. They mourned the death of their big brother and felt our pain as his parents. We sensed a special tenderness as they helped us put in order the leftover pieces of Chris's life.

And they had their own grief. A different kind of grief. The grief of brother for brother — memories of fun and fights, of shared secrets, of kindnesses and slights, knowledge of one another that only brothers and sisters have — all those ingredients that make for a deep sibling love and a sometimes fierce rivalry.

As they moved back into their own lives, I suspect it was with mingled relief and guilt. After all, they were still alive. Their dreams and hopes were not dead, as Chris's were. They could go on trying to live their dreams.

How did I know how they felt? I didn't know for sure, although I did at times sense unspoken thoughts (mothers claim to have that instinct), and once in awhile one of them said something or did something or I heard something from someone else that led me to guess at their feelings.

Their suffering was not unnoticed. We have been conscious of their pain. I hope they feel we have stood by them as they have lived (and undoubtedly are still living) out the confusions of their special sorrows, each in his own way. They have stood by us as we immersed ourselves in a Chris world, sometimes oblivious to them. They must at times have felt we indeed loved Chris more than we loved them. (We know this is not true, but we hope never to have to prove it.) It has been hard for all of us. We think they have been extraordinarily patient with us.

Now, here we all are, going on with our lives without Chris. There are the grandchildren, every one precious to us. Jason, fifteen and growing tall, our only grandson, nine at the time of the tragedy, is in the throes of adolescence. Treva, eight, brown-eyed and musical, and Alison, a graceful seven-year-old señorita, in third and second grades respectively, with permanent teeth growing in conspicuous gaps where baby teeth used to be, read and write real words. Carrie, a five-year-old mischievous imp of a girl now in kindergarten, who loves to draw, and who has never seen her Uncle Chris, tries to keep up. And Jordan, an articulate three-year-old, also born since her Uncle Chris died, charms and cheers us with her winsome personality. And now, at this writing another — a baby brother or sister for Jordan — is on the way to enrich our lives.

The existence of these dear young human beings in our family has brightened our lives and eased the pain. At the same time, they have caused us to look at our imperfect world with worried eyes as we ponder their future.

And then there is Cheri, Tim's wife, an accountant, who has temporarily reduced working time to be a mother twice over; Jeri, Jon's wife, an up-and-coming artist and writer; and Patricia, Ben's wife, a talented pianist and hard-working piano professor, all outstanding daughters-in-law, caring and thoughtful, good to our sons.

And our sons. There were those who were sorry for us as we turned out one boy after the other. "Another boy," they'd say, "You don't know what you're missing." This may be true. It doesn't really matter to us. Who can experience everything in life anyway? Besides, now we have four granddaughters *and* a grandson and another grandchild on the way.

In truth, we were never sorry we didn't have a girl. Certainly, our sons at times led us on scary and uncharted adventures, but they have emerged as handsome and considerate human beings. Tim, the freckle-faced lad with a thousand ideas, now a CPA, is the finance manager of Ambassador Cards, a subsidiary of Hallmark Cards in Kansas City. Jon, the one with blond curly hair as a baby, is an editor with the Correspondence Schools Department at the University of Texas in Austin. Ben, the youngest, always trying to keep up, is the tallest; he is a folk musician and piano technician in Frankfort, Kentucky.

Yes, here we all are. Missing our son, brother, brother-in-law, uncle. Adjusting to a family life without his presence. Aware that we will always carry the memory of his death and who he was within us in some way or other. Doing the best we can with our lives. Perhaps more aware than some of the marvelous gift of life.